THE HEART
IS HIGHLAND

MEMORIES OF A CHILDHOOD IN A SCOTTISH GLEN

For Joan
Best wishes
Maisie.

THE HEART IS HIGHLAND

MEMORIES OF A CHILDHOOD IN A SCOTTISH GLEN

MAISIE STEVEN

breedon **books**
PUBLISHING

DEDICATION

For Ken, who not only encouraged me to value my Highland heritage, but also to write this book.

Also to remember fondly my parents and sister Nancy, and our friends Revd Farquhar and Mrs Barbara Matheson, late of Glen Urquhart.

First published in Great Britain in 2001 by
The Breedon Books Publishing Company Limited
Breedon House, 3 The Parker Centre, Derby, DE21 4SZ.

ISBN 1 85983 222 9

Printed and bound by Butler & Tanner Ltd, Frome, Somerset
Cover printing byGreenShires Ltd, Leicester

CONTENTS

ACKNOWLEDGEMENTS

Sincere thanks are due to the Drummond Trust for their generous grant toward publication. Warm thanks also to my brother-in-law Donald Campbell and to my friends in the glen, Pam Fraser and Chrissie Macdonald, for having gone to considerable trouble to unearth old photographs. And once again I thank my son Ken for providing the inspiration and constant encouragement for the writing of this book.

Maisie Steven
Aberfeldy
Perthshire

INTRODUCTION

This account of my early life would never have been written without the encouragement and persistence of my son Kenneth.

A hard-working poet and writer who never seems to experience the slightest difficulty in picking up a pen, Ken found it hard to understand my reluctance; frankly, I was puzzled myself. On reflection, I decided there were several reasons. Laziness came into it, of course; the task seemed more than a little daunting. There was also some apprehension, a fear of unearthing too many poignant memories – of home, parents, departed friends, and especially of my only sister Nancy, my constant companion of early years. Perhaps there was also real uncertainty as to whether what I could recall would ever be sufficient to give the story life.

Finally I made a very tentative start with the month of January. And then a strange thing happened. As if a cupboard full of old treasures had been opened and the contents spilled out on to the floor, all kinds of memories began to surface – of people, places and events, and of customs and traditions, some of which I had not thought of for over half a century.

So I continued, my pen, as it were, picking up speed as the months came and went. It had been a happy choice, I found, to write keeping time with the months, because the similar environment of rural Perthshire helped to jog my memory. And as each month was written up, Ken, my eagle-eyed but ever-helpful editor, would unerringly point out just where I had strayed into potential boredom – usually when I had mounted my hobby-horse of food habits!

Memories flooded back of the faces and names (and of course the nicknames) of those who had peopled our childhood; some of these were true 'characters' about whom numerous anecdotes surfaced. A miscellany of events also came to mind – the ploughing match, the *ceilidhs*, the Gaelic Mod, tales of the Monster, Sunday School picnics at Urquhart Castle, the fun and excitement of Hallowe'en, and the Communions with all their solemnity.

All of this was proving relatively easy; it was simply a case of seeing it all through the eyes of a child, of recapturing something of a vanished way of life. It became more difficult when there seemed to be a need for more mature appraisal, of the education available to us at the time, for example. There was a need to assess it fairly and honestly, and to try to hammer out a balanced view of the vexed issue of the 'boarded-out' children with whom that education was shared. (I take full responsibility for my possibly flawed impressions and inevitable lapses of memory.)

I did not always need to rely on re-awakened memory, simply because a clear impression had remained from my earliest days. This was true of the natural world. So steeped had we been in the joys of the countryside that it was altogether impossible *not* to remember vividly; the only question was how, lacking the skills of a poet, to express them adequately! All were things of the senses – the sight of a perfect chaffinch's nest with its clutch of minute eggs, or of daffodils against the snow; the sound of bees droning through the heather, or of curlews crying on a May evening; the feel of a warm hen's egg in the hand, or of tiny kittens vibrating with purring as they were fed; the scent of new-mown hay, or of lilac or primroses or lily-of-the-valley; the taste of brambles or hazel-nuts or freshly-made raspberry jam. The

Nancy and Maisie aged four and two.

list seemed endless; in the struggle to convey these delights came a growing awareness of the richness of the childhood we had been privileged to enjoy. I thought with some sadness of the journalist who had written several years before: 'I can't stand the countryside myself – one cow looks just like another to me!'

Re-awakened memory was also totally unnecessary when it came to our musical inheritance, always important to the Gael. Brought up in a musical household, I knew the tunes and the words – or at least the choruses – of dozens of Gaelic and Scots songs; brought up in the Free Church, I was familiar with the words and tunes of a great many psalms. I knew many fiddle and bagpipe tunes. Not only could I recapture details of long-ago *ceilidhs*, I could *hear* the special songs of each performer, for no matter how many new songs they might have learned, by the end of the evening someone would have invariably required them to sing 'their' song!

The whole exercise of recalling the vibrant life of the glen has left a mixture of emotions. Sadness, naturally, for those who are gone; wistfulness for the richness of a lifestyle mercifully free from today's consumerism; sheer gratitude for having been brought up amid great natural beauty, and for the warmth and immense security of a strong home and family life, loving discipline and sound teaching – as well as a great deal of fun. True, the strong religious ethos of the day could be stern and at times repressive, yet the consequence, arguably, was a standard of morality which meant that no door need ever be locked, and a parcel from any shop – even the jeweller's – could be left lying for hours at the roadside to be collected.

It would be a pity if these reminiscences were to be seen as mere nostalgia for the past; better, surely, to take from them something positive for the future. Exactly what that might be is obviously left to the individual reader. For me, what seems to shine through is just how much more quality of life means than standard of living, and how happiness is not, contrary to the message of today's aggressive advertising, dependent upon material possessions. Surely we can choose in different ways to regain that lost simplicity. This idea seems to be summed up in a verse of a poem written by Ken for a young Latvian friend, inspired by a photograph of him, picking potatoes behind a horse.

> If a man should come now to your door
> Selling motorways, a rustle of money in his eyes,
> Do not buy his road, for it leads
> To all our lost riches, our need of God.

Kenneth C. Steven, *A Poem for Ivars*

JANUARY

T HE FEELING of excitement comes back vividly still, after all the years. New Year in the glen was always special. It was like nothing else, not even Christmas, which to us as children was the most exciting day of all. But this was different. We could sense in the grown-ups an underlying excitement, mixed perhaps with a certain solemnity, and it affected us as well.

It would have begun days before, with our mother cleaning the house from end to end, almost like a second spring-cleaning. Maybe for some there was a touch of superstition in it, for one heard remarks such as 'dirty at New Year, dirty all year round', from time to time. But on the great day itself, little work would be done. On the farms and crofts, there would be the animals to feed and the cows to milk; in our own case there were only the hens. But our mother would be busy in the kitchen, preparing the meal that would be served around midday. And what a feast it would be! The smell of a fowl roasting in the oven, or of a plum pudding boiling, is still sufficient to recapture the distinctive atmosphere of the season in a moment.

For my sister Nancy and myself, though, there could at times be some apprehension about the menu. Would it be a hen? And if so, which hen? We had a relatively small flock, usually about 12 to 15 in all, and we *knew* those hens. They were our friends. Most of all we dreaded the demise of 'our' hens; each spring we were allowed to choose one from the cheeping flock newly hatched – usually a black chick from among a majority of yellows – and these became our pets, readily feeding out of our hands. 'Not Jessie!' we would wail in unison, 'We could never, never

Nan at our grandfather's sheep farm – the original Mossford.

eat Jessie!' Although I honestly believe we were normally obedient children, brought up with the strictness customary for the time, we dug in our heels on this particular issue and were, surprisingly, indulged. Perhaps a *coileach* (cockerel) would have the misfortune to be chosen instead. What Jessie's ultimate fate was, I cannot clearly recall.

Some years all might be plain sailing – we might be having pheasant instead. Our father was not averse to shooting the occasional pheasant, or more often a rabbit, from the bedroom window. Or it might be venison. A gamekeeper's son and always a keen shot, our father was often offered 'a day on the hill' by one of his gamekeeper friends in Wester Ross toward the end of the year. The liver and heart would be eaten immediately, while the best part of the haunch would be reserved for New Year. But there might be a piece of liver kept for the cat, a distinct improvement on the staple feline diet of the time – porridge, milk and mice.

When I was 10, new horizons opened up when the family acquired a modest car. A variation on the day's programme then became possible, for we would be invited to visit our maternal grandparents in Dingwall, some 20 miles away. Memories of those visits conjure up a different kind of enjoyment, that of being welcomed as part of a larger clan; if our MacPherson cousins were there along with their parents, as well as our unmarried uncle and aunt, there might be about a dozen in the company. At the huge dining table with its snowy cloth and sparkling silver, Granny would preside at one end, resplendent in her black dress and beautiful gold brooch, while Granda sat very upright at the other, ready to pronounce a lengthy Gaelic blessing on the food – and on us all. It was always good to be there, not least because of the secure, warm feeling of being part of the family, the very youngest there.

Vivid though those memories are, I don't believe that the visits can have taken place all that often, simply because at New Year the whole countryside would so often be in the grip of hard frost. Between ourselves and Dingwall there lay the dreaded Beauly Brae, a road winding up from the glen through a wooded gorge to a height of perhaps 800 feet, with very steep gradients that today's cars would scarcely notice, but which absolutely petrified us then. And if there was snow, or even the slightest possibility of ice, my mother would flatly refuse to go. Nan and I, equally timorous – although never back-seat drivers in the same way – would be mightily relieved, chiefly because of horrendous tales (hopefully apocryphal) of cars that had slipped back and gone over the edge. Our father would have chanced anything.

There was another factor involved; if we stayed at home, there might well be a musical evening, and we loved that too. We did not, incidentally, call such gatherings *ceilidhs*; that term was reserved for informal concerts in the public hall. But essentially 'to *ceilidh*' meant simply to have a long chat – a blether – around the fire. And of that there was plenty at New Year.

One particular aspect of the excitement in the early years comes readily to mind. It was always a thrill, especially at New Year, to have the parlour fire lit. It was of course no novelty to us to have a 'real' fire; the kitchen range warmed the heart of the house all day, every day, while the log fire in the living room was always on from early afternoon. But this was a different thing altogether; the parlour was strictly for Sundays and special occasions. We used to love to tiptoe in, when the fire was going well but the lamps were not yet lit, to savour the atmosphere. It used to seem as if the whole room stood in anticipation of the evening; the piano especially seemed to be standing there with bated breath waiting to be allowed to make music. We would look around to see dancing flames reflected in the highly-polished furniture and the burnished brass fender, or winking in the glasses laid out ready on a tray. Only at this one time, New Year, would there be whisky in the house – a single dram for the men, and a glass of green ginger or port for the women. Children would be given fruit 'wine' or home-made ginger cordial; lemonade, a rare treat, was strictly for summer occasions. Each drink was invariably served with a genteel piece of shortbread. Later, the assembled company would be regaled with tea and sandwiches, scones and black bun. Christmas cake was a much later addition.

When we were very young, we would be tucked up in bed before the party began. It was still exciting, though, to hear our parents' friends arriving, and the cheerful greetings: 'a good New Year to you all!', or more often '*bliadhna mhath ur dhiubh!*' as they were welcomed in, and to have them pop their heads round the bedroom door to greet us too. Very often there would be our good friend Donnie with the 'box' – the button accordion which he played so well – and probably a couple from one of the crofts on the 'heights' with a fiddle and a banjo, as well as two or three others who either played or sang, or simply enjoyed listening to music.

When we were a little older we would be allowed to stay up for the earlier part of the evening. We were always cajoled into singing, but because of our intense shyness, our song would be delivered from the hallway, with the parlour door open – usually a Gaelic duet, or a simple version of Brahms's *Lullaby*. We were fortunate to have a musical inheritance from both sides of the family, so singing came easily. Nan, a contralto, was able to harmonise naturally from an early age.

Then the music would begin – strathspeys, marches and reels; songs in Gaelic, English and Scots; laments, love-songs and lullabies. It has often been said that the Gaels are 'never happier than when they are lamenting.' I have to admit that in our case there was some truth in this – yet surely everyone knows that the sad songs are by far the most beautiful! As for the instrumental music, it was by any standards cheerful enough.

How many are the songs of the Gaels? Are they to be counted in hundreds? Or in thousands? Certainly, our mother, an accomplished singer, had what seemed to us an endless repertoire, which was constantly growing each year as the prescribed songs for the Gaelic Mod were added. In large measure, those songs reflected the tragic history of the Highlanders – songs of eviction and exile, songs recounting the beauties of beloved places never to be seen again, songs of lost loves, war and death. Some were beautiful enough to crush the heart – even as small children we would cry when our mother sang them, despite, at that time, knowing few of the words. One of them stands out in my memory; it seemed to me the most heart-rending and lovely of all, and is still my favourite Gaelic song. *Caisteal a'Ghlinne* (the castle in the glen) tells of an unknown prisoner shut up in a cold dungeon, expressing his sense of hopelessness that nobody will listen to him despite his innocence, and his longing to be back with the one he loves. I believe it dates from the 17th century.

At last, reluctantly, we would go off to bed, to lie listening entranced to the music. It was an amateur performance, but the playing was spirited and the singing was from the heart, and to us it sounded wonderful. Our mother would be at the piano, and there was usually at least one other on the fiddle besides Dad, who also had a fine voice and was precentor of our local Free Church. We would resolve to stay awake to the very end, but it never happened – we would always drift off to sleep to the sound of the music. Altogether it was a fitting end to a happy New Year's Day.

Do not imagine that this was the end of New Year! On the contrary, all was not complete until every friend and neighbour, or indeed every passing acquaintance (or so it seemed), had been in to receive some form of hospitality. Sometimes we would visit, as a family, old friends further afield whom we had perhaps not seen since the previous New Year, to be treated to festive fare and, likely enough, some form of musical entertainment. More often though, we would accompany our mother to the home of some female neighbour, where we would be given books to read or something else to amuse us, while the women talked. But all the time, of course, we were all ears; and we would marvel as the talk went on; the enquiries and replies would not come to an end until every single member of both families had been covered – the married daughter in Edinburgh, the new baby, the uncle in Canada... Our mother was no gossip, we knew; so in the face of possible cynicism I would stoutly maintain that this was a genuine expression of interest and concern, part of the outworking of a deep-seated sense of community. In a day long before the social services on which many depend today, it was certainly required.

Many years later, as a student in Glasgow, I remember trying to describe to my landlady what it was like to live in a Highland glen. 'But it must be so lonely!' was her oft-repeated verdict. Lonely, indeed! As far as I could gather, *she* knew only a few of the people in the surrounding streets, as well as some relatives and friends further afield. (I do not speak, of course, of the tenement dwellers, whose conditions were altogether different.) But *we* knew pretty well everyone in the entire glen – the children we went to school with, their parents and brothers and sisters, people in the shops and the post office, everyone in each house in our own village and many in the surrounding villages, those on the neighbouring crofts and farms, the bus drivers, the van-men... And, well, if we didn't exactly know them all personally, we knew plenty about them!

Inevitably there was gossip. Among the wifies, especially, there would be intense interest in such minutiae of life as what somebody might have paid for a posh new hat, or what a landlady might be charging her lodger, or why somebody was going so often to Inverness on the bus. Doubtless there could be much more cruel gossip at times as well – especially perhaps when an illegitimate child was born; life must have been incredibly hard for some girls, for it was they who had to bear the brunt of the situation. Certain habitual drunks would also be the subject of talk, although there could also be a tolerant attitude that now seems remarkable; I can easily recall how, when we would be listening in to grown-up talk, we would prick up our ears as the voices dropped and we would hear some man (and in those days it would always be a man) described as being 'foolish' – the accepted euphemism of the day. There was also speculation about possible marriages among those young folk known to be going out together. Later, as we grew up, all of this began to jar; we would gladly have settled for the anonymity of the town. It probably took the experience of sheer city loneliness to change our views.

All that has been said above primarily concerns the celebratory side of New Year, but there was also a serious side. On the first Sunday of the year we would go, as always, as a family to church. On those occasions when New Year's Day actually fell on a Sunday, festivities (apart perhaps from a rather more lavish than usual dinner, prepared the day before) would have to be postponed till the Monday – certainly in a Free Church household like ours. Even if Sunday came as late as 5 or 6 January, there would still be an orgy of greetings and hearty handshaking after the Gaelic service (we went in as they came out), and then again afterwards; we learned to dread the pumping of our small hands by the large gnarled ones of some of the crofters! But beyond it all, I am certain that the same sense of community, the warm feeling of belonging, was strongly present as well.

It would have been difficult, if not impossible, to grow up in the Free Church without having it instilled into one that life is to be taken seriously. Perhaps this was particularly true at New Year. The service was always well over an hour, nor was there in those days the special concession of a children's address, or of being allowed to troop out to Sunday School! Naturally we found it long; we were by no means above inventing games to help pass the time – like counting the number of coloured hats worn by the women versus the more favoured black ones. Many of the older women dressed entirely in black; these we irreverently called 'the crows'. Having to sit still was a discipline, though, and even if we chafed, I doubt whether we actually knew the word 'bored' in those days – by and large it was something we simply accepted; and inattentive though we were, I believe the message did reach us that New Year is a significant, even a solemn time, for looking back and looking forward. We would be reminded that some who had been there last year were there no longer; some present today might well not be there next New Year; the year before us was held in the hands of God, and our only security lay in Him. We were *never* permitted to say 'we'll do that in May', or even: 'I'll see you next Monday'. Those who could not quite bring themselves to say 'God willing' could at least be expected to manage 'if all's well'. To this day it makes me uneasy to hear anyone confidently predict their future activities.

'Old New Year' was on 12 January. By then we realised the festive season was virtually at an end. It was always a sad thing to take the holly down; in the early days we didn't have much else – paper chains and tinsel came later. But in any case it was the holly that mattered; we hated to see it go. For a few days we would be disconsolate, feeling that all the fun, the parties and the visiting had come to an end, and life was dull. But then something would happen to change our perspective completely. Perhaps there would be snow. Often, though, there would come in mid-January a day released early from spring, a day with that indefinable feeling of the promise of things to come. Then, forgetting all indoor amusements, we would clamour to be out – it was as if the real core of our lives was always out-of-doors – and, released, we would be racing to the top of the garden, desperate to see if the snowdrops were coming up in their special place under the high wall that separated us from the garden of the big hotel next door. And sure enough, there they would be!

It is hard not to appear to exaggerate in expressing what the snowdrops meant to us. Although we did not actually belong to the farming and crofting community, we were all the same acutely aware of the rhythm of the seasons and their activities – the ploughing, the harrowing, the sowing, the potato planting, the various harvests – but, especially, we were involved in the productions of our own large and fertile garden. Not that we could have been classed as keen gardeners! Indeed, I wonder whether teaching children skills like pricking out small plants, or even pruning, would not arouse their interest more than the mundane weeding and clearing of stones which fell to our lot? But the snowdrops... nothing, we felt, could ever be as exciting as those first brave green shoots pushing up, to remind us that spring was on the way. Sometimes we would search to find them under several inches of snow, and that was even more of a thrill. And we would always feel thankful that at least they had a warm blanket to cover them.

Having renewed acquaintance with the earth after a longish lapse of

Drumnadrochit village in the 1930s.

time, we would be impatient to use the spring-like day to explore further. Away we would go up the field that went steeply up from our back fence (always, though, having first asked permission; we were never allowed simply to disappear). At the top of the field was a wood, a magical place. But on this occasion we might well by-pass it to climb to the top of the second field, which took us high enough to look down upon the whole wide glen spread below, the fields that yellowish-green so reminiscent of January days. What we wanted to see most of all was the loch; from our east-facing windows we could barely catch a glimpse of it; but now it could be clearly seen, spread out like a dark shining mirror. We could pick out the two rivers, the Enerick and the Coilty, flowing through the villages of Drumnadrochit and Lewiston respectively, like black snakes as they appeared from time to time among the trees, making their way to Loch Ness. A stand of sombre-looking yews marked the glen's ancient burial-place. Dominating the view to the south-west was the pudding-shaped bulk of Meallfourvonie, more than 2,000 feet high. We would plan the expedition we would have one day, to climb it and perhaps see the *whole* of Loch Ness from there... sadly, it was to be at least 20 years before it happened.

More than anything else, we simply loved to stand there and drink in the whole scene. It was *our* place. People have since asked me whether children brought up in beautiful places really appreciate the beauty around them. I have no hesitation in saying that we certainly did. Perhaps I should add, though, that in our case awareness was encouraged by our parents. They had spent their first three years of marriage in a flat in a southern industrial town, where our mother pined for a garden and our father for the hills, and they were acutely conscious of the privilege of living in a Highland glen. They passed these sentiments on to us, teaching us to appreciate every aspect of country living. As the year went by, it was as though picture after picture became indelibly imprinted on our minds, pictures that would, in later years, be treasured, brought out and polished, always kept fresh.

I remember January as a time when illness often struck; flu and other epidemics would ravage the community. The dread of pneumonia, in particular, was impressed upon our minds early through oft-repeated 'case histories' of the disease. Like many other housewives of the time, our mother had had to acquire skills in home nursing, employing a whole range of remedies – poultices, inhalation and bed baths – unfamiliar to a generation accustomed to being treated with a whole pharmacopoeia of drugs. Possibly it was due to her excellent care and skill, and perhaps the extra attention, but I tend to recall being ill as a predominantly pleasant experience. There was one outstanding feature which did, I am sure, contribute to this – a fire in the bedroom! Our house was a bungalow, fairly novel for the time and only the second built in the glen, and although modern, it still had some of the older features, including a fireplace in every room. What I remember most vividly is the sensation of waking up fevered during the night, feeling reduced to a tiny speck, with

Loch Ness and the road to Fort Augustus before the war.

Nancy, Maisie and friend with toys in the garden at Mossford.

the ceiling seemingly miles above. It was a state that could give rise to a sense of panic, but the comforting flicker of flames reflected on the ceiling, with their companionable warmth, would gradually bring peace, and lull one back to sleep.

If being ill could actually be enjoyable, being given medicine – generally speaking at least – could be quite horrendous! The prevailing maxim, I feel sure, was that if a cure didn't taste bad, it couldn't possibly be effective. In a class of its own, undoubtedly, was the cure-all of the day – castor oil. We used to dread, when we had the flu, seeing our mother coming in with a small glass of orange juice, in the bottom of which was a centimetre or so of clear (ugh) oil – because of course the two didn't mix; all that resulted from her well-intentioned efforts was that we were put off orange juice for years! A friend who had been in hospital with appendicitis told us that the very first thing that happened there, no matter what you were suffering from, was that you were dosed with castor oil; fortunately we never did have cause to verify that!

To be fair, many of the other medicines were tolerable in comparison – except for one dreadful laxative called *cascara sagrada* (*cascara evacuant*, on the other hand, was acceptable enough). For some reason there was great emphasis in those days on laxatives; we were regularly dosed with syrup-of-figs, which fortunately was sweet and fairly popular with children.

Nancy and Maisie in their early teens, with mother outside Mossford.

Our mother was a great believer in dietary supplements, chief of which was cod liver oil. Fortunately for me, I was able to take this 'neat' without flinching; Nan was not, so eventually we had the oil in emulsion form. Then there was malt extract – sweet and toffee-like, and in great

The glen, looking south-west to Meallfourvonie – the view from the top of 'our' field.

demand. In addition, every spring we would be dosed with a mixture of sulphur and treacle to 'clean the blood', usually followed by a course of an iron tonic called Parrish's Food – palatable enough, but a great nuisance in that it was necessary to brush one's teeth afterwards.

Dr Macdonald, our local GP, did all his own dispensing, and we used to be fascinated by the array of phials and bottles in his consulting room. After even a simple illness everyone expected to receive a 'tonic' – usually coloured green or red. 'Did you get a bottle?' people would ask each other after a visit to the doctor; there was something wrong if you missed out!

The month would be nearing its close, as I remember, when one event of immense importance to the local housewives would take place. This was The Making of the Marmalade. Let no one imagine this is any kind of exaggeration! On the contrary, it was the first instalment of the annual domestic work cycle. Let no one think, either, that this represented the production of a mere dozen or so pots of preserve; in our house perhaps 80–100 pounds would be made, to be stored either in two-pound jars, or in large earthenware crocks.

The outlay of energy in this highly labour-intensive process was quite prodigious. But there was, in our glen, one redeeming feature; the owner of the village's main shop was generous enough to lend out his bacon-cutting machine to assist housewives with cutting the peel. In a day of few labour-saving devices, this gesture was deeply appreciated. When it was our mother's turn for the cutter, we would arrive home from school to find the kitchen transformed into a mini-factory, the house filled with the inimitable citrus aroma. Successive boilings in the big brass jelly-pan would be required before, tired but triumphant, she would have whole shelves in the larder filled with rows of jars of delicious marmalade, neatly covered with circles of white gummed paper, each tidily named and with the date added (as if any, given away as they so often were, had a hope of surviving to the following year!).

The sequel to this episode has to be told. Needless to say, we took this excellent marmalade totally for granted. One year we went on holiday to Ullapool, staying, as the custom then was, in a house offering 'rooms with full board'. Each day at breakfast we had morning rolls – a novelty to us then; but we also had something that was an even greater novelty – Silver Shred marmalade. Never, we decided, had we tasted anything as delicious. Poor mother!

FEBRUARY

SNOW! Could there possibly be a more suitable or exciting way to start the month traditionally known as 'February-fill-the-dykes'? None, certainly, that Nan and I could have wished for. Snow was always a delight. The only thing we couldn't agree on was which we loved more – to stand at the window watching the big flakes fall (our hearts would always sink if our parents assured each other that the ground was too wet and it wouldn't lie) or to wake up in the morning to that strange kind of light, and a white world? Perhaps, just slightly, we favoured the latter with its element of surprise. The beauty of the trees, especially, always bowled us over; in the accepted cliché of the day, we would tell each other that they were 'like fairy lacework'. In the glen, clichés were an unselfconscious part of everyone's speech; it was as invariably 'as good as gold', or 'as happy as a sandboy' – whatever that may have meant. But in school, when writing an essay, we would not have dared to use such expressions.

In an area where serious consequences could follow heavy snowstorms, our delight would often be tinged with guilt; we would hear our father telling of somebody's sheep having to be dug out of a deep drift, or of remote farms or crofts cut off. Deep down, though, we would simply be wishing it had been us – the joy of being cut off from school! In all our schooldays, it never did happen. And in a school as geared to academic effort and sheer hard slog as ours, I scarcely recall ever being sent home an hour early because of snow.

Whatever the depth of the snow, suffice it to say we would be desperate to be out, to make the most of it – this being largely determined by the consistency of the snow. If it was of the kind that packed easily, our mother must have learned to expect us home late, liberally caked with the stuff, having sustained a battering from the boys on the way. Try as we might, we never did succeed in throwing straight; we were never anything like a match for them! Once, after school, a boy in my class sent a snowball (with a stone inside it, which was even worse) crashing through one of the school windows. The fact that he, poor soul, was related to the headmaster did nothing to save him from the inevitable belting – rather the reverse.

At one time we were given a proper sledge by family friends. Although this was a much-appreciated gift, the trouble was that it wouldn't always work; the snow might be too deep, or too wet and slushy, or there wasn't a sufficient covering. On those occasions the old tin tray that we had always used, and which was really our favourite, would come into its own again. With deep snow which 'stuck', we would set to work like a pair of navvies and beat it down until we had a smooth shining track that was wickedly fast. In the middle of 'our' field there was a kind of hummock, below which the ground fell away quite sharply. We would hurtle down the last bit, to crash into the fence backwards, helpless with laughter. Making a snowman in the garden was enjoyable, but tame in comparison.

We didn't feel the cold during these winter expeditions and were certainly at no risk of hypothermia! I still shudder to think of all the woollen garments we wore (especially under-garments, the most horrendous of which were hairy 'combinations'). On top of the outer clothes, a huge scarf would be wound round our necks and then our middles, and fastened behind with a safety pin. Thus fortified, we could have stayed out for hours; sadly, though, it never seemed to happen; after what would seem to us like a few minutes, we would be called in to begin the all-important 'lessons' – the word always used for homework.

Very low temperatures, and especially ice, could lead to even greater hazards than snow. On the roads, sand would sometimes be shovelled, manually, from a lorry; for much of the time, though, roads would go untreated. On our father's periodic shooting trips to the west, he would be cajoled (or more often coerced) into fitting chains on to the tyres – a process he hated, but which might well have saved accidents. Once, when he went without these, he turned the car over just above the notorious Rogie Falls between Contin and Garve, and was only stopped by a couple of rowan trees. This episode was played down as 'landing in a ditch' until the true story came out years later.

Inside the house, keeping a keen frost at bay in those pre-central heating days could be a nightmare, requiring a paraffin heater in the hallway and tiny lamps burning at vulnerable points such as U-bends. Despite the heat of the kitchen range and extra fires, the cold in most houses was of a degree few would begin to tolerate today. I recall the wry comment of my Glasgow landlady: 'My toes are always warm but my heels are cold!'

The annual Ploughing Match.

What we did have was the joy of a roaring fire of logs and coal; our father was a wonderful fire-maker, with a special method that ensured long-lasting heat. His fires, known as 'Dad's scorchers', were carefully built with a log at each side, coal in the middle and dross at the back. There cannot be many domestic joys greater than that of sitting at a really good fire; the only drawback was that, if you sat too near, you got *breacan teine* (fire tartan) – red marks on the front of your legs. Also, even the thought of facing a freezing corridor, or an arctic bedroom, was a real challenge.

Ice outside the house was emphatically to be enjoyed. At school there would always be a slide – a long, ferocious one in the boys' playground, a more sedate one in ours. Yet to small timid girls it could seem daunting enough; we stood in line, and when our turn came, had to launch ourselves on to the ice, often quite scared, but much more worried about showing even the slightest sign of fear. Once, Nan and I went up to the top of the hill behind our house, where there was a fairly large farm; the attraction was their pig, for which we used to gather acorns. The son of the house, one of the 'big boys', was there that day. He came sliding down the farm track, which was completely covered in thick ice, nonchalant and relaxed in his tackety boots, with their metal studs for grip, kept steady by a stable broom held in front of him. We were speechless with shyness and admiration; never had we seen such a slide.

If memory serves correctly, it was in February that the annual Ploughing Match took place; possibly the date varied according to whether the weather was suitable or not. Just how far back this local event went it is difficult to say, but it seems unlikely that the glen's version was as old as the first 'Plowing Match' recorded in the Old Statistical Account as having been held in East Lothian in 1784! My own earliest memory of it is extremely vivid; it is of sitting perched on our front gate as 'Andack' passed along with his splendid pair of Clydesdales, on his way to Jock Tolmie's field. The horses were decorated from harness to tail with gaily-coloured ribbons and bells; spellbound, I would not be moved until I was sure that every single horse had passed.

We would always be desperate to go to watch the ploughing early, but my memory is of having to wait until the afternoon before joining the rest of the populace walking round and marvelling at the straightness of the furrows. While the attendant flock of gulls were enjoying their tasty morsels, we would be enjoying ours – in this instance hot sausage rolls, quite a novelty to us in those days.

The prize-giving was of course awaited with the keenest interest. Everyone knew who the best ploughmen were, and the competition was fierce. There could have been disappointment – and doubtless there sometimes was – but the real thoughtfulness of the committee who drew up the prize-list ensured that few competitors were left without some reward. Apart from the coveted prize for excellence, there would be one for the ploughman with the biggest family or the best-decorated pair of horses, as well as for the shortest, the tallest, the best Gaelic speaker... and so on. It is hard to convey to those unfamiliar with such events just how much enthusiasm was generated by this single gathering; in addition it must have done a great deal to ensure the passing on of highly-valued skills to each new generation.

There would be a kind of sequel the following week, as we re-lived the excitement by poring over the results in the *Inverness Courier*. And then a recurrent problem would surface – the distinguishing of names. First prize, Donald Fraser. Now which Donald Fraser would that be? Or Alec MacDonald? Because of the great preponderance of Frasers and MacDonalds in the glen, it was imperative that they be given some other name – and there was no lack of those. Some would of course be known by the name of their crofts or farms; a whole tribe of children might have their father's Christian name tacked on to their own; someone might be known by hair colour (*ruadh* (red) would be an obvious example). But some had true nicknames, the most bizarre of which come readily to mind. Why on earth, we used to wonder, would somebody have been known as 'Donnie Bagsalt', 'Danny Caesar', or 'Willie Winks'? The origins were perhaps long since forgotten. But just occasionally, some unfortunate newcomer would fall into the trap of actually addressing someone by his or her nickname, and the story of the *faux pas* would be told gleefully round the glen.

Apart from the numerous Frasers and MacDonalds, there were of course representatives of other clans – families of Grants, MacDougalls, MacMillans, MacLeans, MacKenzies, MacLeods, Munros, Camerons, Campbells, Rosses and Chisholms; there were also quite a number of our own name, MacKintosh. One day Nan and I were passed as we walked along the road by a lady on a bicycle. She dismounted, turned back to us and in an accent unfamiliar to us at the time said 'Excuse me, but did you happen to see a mackintosh on the road?' We looked at her uncertainly for a moment and then ventured hesitantly: 'Well, we're MacKintoshes.' Realising our mistake at once, we burst out laughing. The lady was not amused; remounting her bicycle, she simply said: 'I have dropped my best mackintosh on the road somewhere'. I remember distinctly that we had to sit on a dyke until we had stopped laughing. In explanation (or in our defence) I should add that in the Highlands we always referred to waterproofs, not mackintoshes.

The fact that February was my birthday month added an extra dimension for me – not that great things could be expected in the way of presents. We might dream of a camera or a watch, perhaps, but we knew quite well we were unlikely to get one. We were not well off by today's standards; although we had everything we needed, there was little room for luxuries. I wonder now whether we ever felt deprived, and if we were aware of the blessings we had – a good home life, plenty of food, warm clothing and, above all, security and constant loving care. Did we take all of these for granted? I believe we did. I do recall, for instance, finding it irksome to wear hand-me-down clothes. I used to wish I had been the older sister. But nearly everyone else was equally poor, and some more so. One thing I do know is that not having luxuries made us truly appreciative of the single, modest gift we did receive on our birthday, and I can easily recall them to this day. Things for which there was a current craze were always the most exciting, such as a yo-yo, a skipping-rope and an autograph book.

These last were very popular in our school. If they had been reserved for famous people, they would never have been used at all! As it was, they were passed round the members of our class for whatever contributions they – or their older sisters or brothers, or even occasionally parents – could produce. Those who were good at art were greatly in demand; others fell back on verses or quotations, or nonsense items like 'picture of a white cat in the snow'. Inevitably someone would squeeze in, at the front or back, 'by hook or by crook, I'll be first/last in your book'. An all-time favourite was:

Can't think, brain numb
Inspiration won't come
Bad ink, worse pen
In desperation, Amen.

A few blots of ink were added to underline the message!

So much for our 'formal' present. We almost never saw a birthday card. But there was one other special feature of our birthdays – something that ran counter to all the general rules laid down by a strict mother – which was that we were allowed to eat (raw) a couple of cubes of packet jelly, or to eat with a spoon, over two or three days, the very smallest tin of sweetened condensed milk. Normally we had no sweets. We were given pocket money only on those rare occasions when we went to Inverness for the day; if family friends brought chocolates, they were dished out one at a time after a meal. So this was absolute bliss to us.

Birthday parties happened very seldom. I remember one when I was 10, chiefly because of having my very first iced cake, with 'Maisie 10' in silver balls on the top. Parties were very simple affairs, with perhaps half a dozen friends – always girls – invited to tea. There would be the inevitable scones and pancakes (which our mother could have produced in her sleep), but with notable additions – our favourite banana sandwiches and, the greatest treat to us, chocolate finger biscuits; there was even a special dish for these. Also adding to the sense of occasion, we would use the silver tea-knives with scarlet handles, which Nan and I thought fit for a laird's table. Following this there would be parlour games – hunt the thimble, blind man's buff, or those requiring paper and pencil, such as consequences, in which we used local characters and amused ourselves hugely with our own wit. It was a treat, too, to have even a single balloon to toss about – until the inevitable happened.

Snowdrops were, of course, my birthday flowers. Earlier, I attempted to convey something of the intensity of our feelings of delight when we saw their green shoots pushing bravely through the ground (or the snow) in January; now, when they were actually in bloom, this was if anything increased. We would be sent up to 'our' wood to gather moss – needless to say, we knew just where to find it – and then the special snowdrop bowl would be brought out, and it was our job to prick holes in the moss with a skewer so that the delicate blooms, with their wonderful mossy, earthy scent, could stand proudly as if growing there. They would grace the table at my birthday tea.

Few people in those days had anything like the number of bulbs commonly grown today; most had just a small patch of snowdrops in a corner of their garden. So it was a thrill for us to go to a certain place where they grew in their hundreds. We would plead with our mother to come and see them with us, and without any great reluctance she would agree. They grew halfway up the long driveway to Drumbuie House, about half a mile away. We did not of course dare to walk up this private drive, but fortunately a farm track ran up the hill parallel to it, with only a burn in between; from there, we were easily able to feast our eyes upon the snowdrops.

It strikes me now that in those days, long before television, sights of this kind constituted our 'viewing'. Members of the family would urge each other to 'come and see' a rainbow; an exotic moth or butterfly; a squirrel eating a nut; a tree whose every twig was weighed down with snow; a beautiful sunset, or massed blooms such as the snowdrops. Less spectacular perhaps than the multitude of scenes available for children's viewing today, but lived at first-hand, and exciting and satisfying to us.

Many years later I was a patient at a Glasgow hospital. Someone had brought me a bunch of white lilac, and one of the young nurses on the ward came over to admire the flowers. 'Are these snowdrops?' she asked. The remark almost made me weep – to think anybody could be so deprived! Somehow for me this was one of those seemingly trivial, yet truly significant moments, startling me into reflecting quite deeply about the richness of the childhood I had been fortunate enough to enjoy.

There would be indoor blooms, too, at the time of my birthday. In today's warmer houses, bulbs planted in September may be expected to flower in time for Christmas; in our childhood February or even March would see them reaching perfection, filling the rooms with their fragrance. This is the time I still deliberately aim for; somehow it seems more appropriate to allow holly, jasmine and Christmas roses to hold sway at Christmas. By early spring, though, one is ready for hyacinths and tulips. To my flower-loving mother, spring would have been incomplete without these; in addition to those mentioned, I was sometimes allowed to grow jonquils, which are still my prime favourites, with their heavy perfume.

One of the more unlikely consequences of the war was that, with Holland an occupied country, the usual bulbs were no longer obtainable. My mother and her friends, I recall, discovered a somewhat bizarre substitute known as 'coalie flowers'. Over some pieces of coal arranged in a bulb bowl was poured a mixture of ink (violet and green gave the best result) and some unknown chemical. The 'flowers' grew as a kind of excrescence on the surface of the coal, and were pretty enough; they could never, of course, take the place of our beloved hyacinths.

In growing these, however, my mother had an ulterior motive as well, for the blooms – provided they were sufficiently presentable, and of more or less regular size and shape – would be entered for a competition at the Women's Rural Institute (WRI), of which she was an enthusiastic member. Week in, week out, there seemed to be a competition of some kind – not, of course, to be taken too seriously. The range was endless; it could be anything from a well-turned knitted sock heel to a cream sponge; from a crocheted collar to a jar of marmalade, jelly or chutney. Or, bearing in mind that those were the days of 'make-do and mend', it could be anything from a child's dress made out of an old coat, to a 're-blocked' hat. The number of demonstrations appeared to be endless. How speakers and demonstrators were found for rural, often remote, areas is hard to understand, but found they were. Some were local people, but for those who came from elsewhere, hospitality would be provided; from time to time someone stayed with us. It would certainly seem fitting here to pay tribute to the sterling work done by the 'Rural' over many years (and perhaps especially during the years of the war) in a huge variety of ways in rural Scotland, not only in raising domestic standards but also in providing wholesome entertainment for many who might otherwise have been extremely isolated.

There were, I believe, two main reasons why spring flowers were so highly prized by us. The obvious one is simply that they were in short supply; in the early barren time of the year, any flowers – even tiny daisies appearing in the grass of a fallow field – were cheering and precious, although by summer gardens, hedgerows and ditches would be filled with a hundred varieties. In addition, I vividly recall something which, at a certain stage in school, was significant for us. In one class, when we were perhaps seven or eight, we had a special kind of drawing-book, with dark brown pages separated by wax sheets. As the teacher brought in flower after flower, we were required to draw them carefully with our crayons (not for us the ease of felt-tipped pens!). In this simple way, the individual beauty of them was, I believe, indelibly stamped upon our minds, along with those minute details that ordinarily we would have been unlikely to notice. Slowly we learned to look for and attempt to reproduce the delicate green fringes on the sepals of snowdrops; the flamboyant orange stamens of crocuses; the slender pink stems of primroses; the rich golden trumpets of daffodils; the scarlet 'eyes' of pheasant-eyed narcissi; the exquisite tiny blue bells of wild hyacinths; the slender leaves of wood anemones ('wooden enemies', as a boy in my class called them, and our family still calls them!). Nor did that teacher neglect the trees; we also struggled to draw the hazel 'lamb's tail' catkins and pussy willows, which we all loved, as well as the buds – and later the leaves – of the commoner trees: birch, rowan, gean, ash, oak and horse chestnut. In spring the wonderful fresh green of the larch gave intense pleasure but was a challenge to draw. Later, in autumn, we would learn in the same way about the various nuts and 'winged' seeds; while they too were exciting, the more lasting impression was created by the new green things of spring.

There was indeed beauty all around us. We would find gossamer spider's webs in which dewdrops caught the sunlight in rainbow hues; dark green mosses with what looked like hundreds of miniscule trees stitched together into a mini-forest; decayed leaves in winter, of which only the marvellously beautiful, intricate web of veins remained. I wonder whether we would have appreciated it all, had we not been taught such reverent observation. We were being taught all the time (if we were really listening) a great deal about the wonders of creation, and concurrently of their Creator. We got what was called 'religious instruction' not only at school, but also at home, and in both church and Sunday school. There was little excuse for not knowing the difference between right and wrong.

Each February the Communion season in the churches brought the 'Sacrament Holidays', when schools would be closed for a statutory five days. This ended during the war, when extra time was given to 'potato holidays'. They were not true holidays – at least not for the children of Free Church and United Free families; by the time we had reached our teens we were required to attend church on Thursday and Friday morning and evening, Saturday morning, Sunday morning and evening, and Monday evening. On Thursday the shops would be closed and it was known as the Fast Day, although the day was more like an ordinary Sunday, with somewhat better food than usual.

At this distance it is not altogether easy to reproduce our early attitudes to this special time in the life of the Church; however, it might be said that we Free Church children had a rather ambivalent attitude. On the one hand, we undoubtedly envied the more relaxed approach of those families who belonged to the 'Established Church'; their children, generally speaking, did indeed have a holiday and were allowed out to play! On the other hand, we tended to to feel superior – obviously, *our* church took the whole occasion with the utmost seriousness, and was therefore 'a right church'.

In those days, a great many people would come to attend the services, from the surrounding districts and also in some cases from quite far afield; this meant that we might have a number of impromptu guests for a meal on the Fast Day or following the Sabbath Communion service. This was something of an excitement for us. More than once at the time of the February Communion, I recall our entertaining folk who had walked several miles in the snow to be there. For my mother, making sure that they had a hearty dinner was clearly a source of satisfaction.

MARCH

'WILL IT COME in like a lion or a lamb?' This question was often asked with a real sense of anxiety as the beginning of March approached. And in an area in which the elements – whether snow, gales or floods – could have serious consequences, this was altogether understandable.

In early spring, and especially with the melting of heavy snow, it was quite customary for the two rivers, the Enerick and the Coilty, to burst their banks. As they flowed through the villages of Drumnadrochit and Lewiston respectively, many of the houses would be badly flooded. Two normally tame and shallow rivers would be transformed, sometimes overnight, into wicked, raging torrents carrying away everything – including livestock – in their path. One year (after we had left school) the Pitkerrald Bridge, an important link between Milton – the most westerly of the glen's triad of villages – and the main road through the Great Glen, was washed away. As it was used by the 'scholars' (our word for pupils) as well as farmers and others, its loss was keenly felt.

During the flood, some children would necessarily be absent from school. On their return they would have harrowing tales to tell of families being forced to live upstairs while lower floors were under water. We and the others not involved would feel, on the one hand, grateful that our homes stood high above the rivers; on the other hand, though, we would inevitably be more than a little envious, because of the high drama of our fellow-pupils' adventures.

On only one occasion, I remember, was the main road between us and the school flooded to such an extent that we could not reasonably be expected to attend. It must have been before we acquired a car, for I distinctly remember our jubilation that morning – and how it was suddenly cut short when the father of one of our friends arrived to give us a lift in his powerful Riley! Never was a kindly-intentioned act accepted with less enthusiasm; needless to say, we were duly despatched by our mother with strict instructions to show no hint of displeasure, but to thank him most politely.

Gales, too, would ravage the glen from time to time, often bringing down trees. There was a line of huge elms and oaks all the way from Drumnadrochit Hotel to Temple Pier by Loch Ness, and one of these stood at either side of our house; many a time we 'measured' them with our eye, debating seriously whether there was any likelihood of one of them hitting us should they happen to fall. The oak still stands there more than half a century on. The elm, sadly, succumbed to disease.

Memory also brings back a very different picture of certain days in March, when the weather would change completely, bringing a sudden heart-warming breakthrough into spring. One hears the expression 'full of the joys of spring' – and that is exactly what March would be to us then, with new life literally bursting out all over. The crocuses would be out in

Mossford, my parents' house in Drumnadrochit. It was only the second bungalow to have been built in the glen.

their glorious colours, and the daffodils coming up – or even in bloom if the winter had been a mild one. It was exciting to see the buds on all the trees; our special favourites were the fat sticky ones of the horse chestnut. There would also be unmistakable signs that the birds were already busy with their nests. For me the most abiding memory of those early spring days is of a mavis (song thrush) singing its heart out from the trees in the hotel garden next door, while my parents were hard at work in the garden.

What a power of work they would put into the garden each spring! The catalogues from Howden's in Inverness would have been thoroughly gone over long before, and the potatoes laid out for sprouting. Our garden was extensive, and very productive; by today's standards we were incredibly self-sufficient. Although flowers had an important place, especially for my mother – she had inherited the greenest of fingers from her father, a head gardener on an estate for many years – our garden existed primarily for the production of food. There was a small lawn to the front and a long paling covered with climbing roses, a fine herbaceous border and some smaller flower beds; the rest, apart from an ample hen-run, was reserved for fruit and vegetables. It need hardly be said that these were organically grown! Although Nan and I tended to wrinkle our fastidious noses when the inevitable load of farmyard dung arrived, we knew it was important. Poultry dung from the hens was also used. There was plenty of fruit – apples and plums, an enclosure with raspberries, a fair-sized strawberry bed, and a large section for black and red currants, and gooseberries and rhubarb. This was all beautifully kept, without any outside help at all. When the ground was first bought, it was a stack yard. Our grandfather came and helped to lay out the garden at that time.

Recently I returned to look at what had been the garden. As the house had been a guest house for some years, a sizeable portion had been made into a parking area; for the rest, it was beautifully landscaped, with lawns and shrubs; one of the old apple trees and a plum tree remained. It looked extremely attractive, but like so many gardens today, produced next to nothing.

In March, then, the garden would be a hive of activity as the ground was prepared for planting. Our own negligible contribution was to gather pail after pail of stones – a job we did with bad grace, feeling at times that the ground grew stones!

I cannot be certain whether we ever bought vegetables, apart from tomatoes from the local shop. We did buy a supplementary supply of onions from the 'Onion Johnny' who came each year from Brittany. From the garden came a regular supply of cabbages, Brussels sprouts,

Maisie and Nan with hens and cat.

cauliflowers, leeks, spring onions, onions, carrots, turnips, swedes, beans, peas, parsnips, beetroot, lettuces and radishes. And, of course, potatoes, although they too were supplemented by our having a 'dreel' (drill) in a field – they played such an important part in our diet. Herbs were not greatly used in traditional Highland cookery; as I recall, we grew only parsley, mint and chives.

It was not only the green growing things that claimed our attention in March. In the fields all around there would be lambs – the black-faced hill sheep would have theirs much later – and some years there would be sheep and lambs in 'our' field; as only a wire fence separated them from us, we could watch them with ease. Repeatedly we were told not to try to catch, or even touch, a lamb; repeatedly we disobeyed. We simply couldn't resist the temptation, if one happened to be lying asleep just through the fence, of sticking our hands through and stroking it. We always expected its 'fur' to be soft like that of our cat; it was disappointing to find instead those tight hard curls! Having achieved our end, we would then be stricken with guilt in case its mother would now refuse to accept it; we would wait anxiously until we had seen them re-united, breathing a sigh of relief that our human scent had not turned the mother sheep off... and then touch a lamb again whenever the chance presented itself.

And then, of course, there were the hens! It is difficult to convey just what a large part these played in our lives when we were very young, especially at the time of the hatching of chicks. Probably if we had been brought up on a farm or croft, with many other animals around us, it would have been different; as it was, they were a constant source of interest to us.

By March, having been 'off the lay' during the winter months, they would be well into their productive stage again. The really strange thing was that in some years, after no eggs had been laid for several weeks, we would suddenly find two or three – almost as if, Nan and I used to think, the hens had held some sort of meeting and decided the right time had come! Then one or two hens would become 'clocken' (broody) and our mother would select the one most likely to make a good mother; she would be housed cosily in a coop lined with straw, surrounded by a fair-sized run protected by wire netting. There she would sit on perhaps 12 or more eggs, in splendid isolation, being disturbed only to be given food and water, which she appeared to accept with reluctance, her mind being taken up with more serious things.

We also had an intense interest in the adult flock. We were a little scared of the strutting *coileach* (cockerel), which was not averse to running at us with menace at times; we left him severely alone. But we loved to feed the hens, particularly those that had become pets and would eat from our hands. Each day a hot mash was prepared for them, which consisted mainly of the smallest potatoes – the *troicheans* (dwarfs), mixed with household scraps and meal. This was their main meal; for the rest, they had Indian corn, and we liked especially to feed this to them. Sometimes, instead of just scattering it, we would place little heaps all over the hen-run, for the sheer pleasure of watching the hens run excitedly from heap to heap, cackling with delight when they found one. Once in a while we would do something really risky; our special pets were easily caught, and we would carry one to the corn barrel for a treat. There it would peck at such a prodigious rate that even we realised it could be dangerous – it would, if given the chance, eat till its crop (in which we could actually feel the corn) was full to bursting. We would remove it after just a few seconds of total bliss and return it to the flock.

Best of all was going to collect the eggs; at times we had to be restrained from rushing to the row of straw-lined nesting boxes (attached to the exterior of the hen-house, but reached by the hens from inside) each time we heard the series of triumphant cackles which announced that an egg had been laid. A warm, newly laid egg in the hand is something very special. It was comparatively tame, all the same, to collect the eggs from a straightforward row of nesting boxes in a hen-house; far more exciting were the times when one actually had to search for them. Our hens were of course free range; a small opening allowed them access to the field, except in those years when there was the possibility that corn was growing there. Occasionally they would 'lay away'; then eggs might be found up in the wood, always, it seemed, in an uncomfortable place for us, under a bramble bush or near a patch of nettles. Still, we would retrieve them, immediately shaking them to determine their freshness – if they rattled, we had found them too late!

From time to time, on a visit to a croft, we would be allowed to go for the eggs, and that was really exciting. They might be found in all manner of hiding places – not just nesting boxes but old barrels, cardboard cartons, even an ancient armchair long since discarded. Under those conditions it was quite a triumph to return with a full basket.

There was one particular duty at home that fell to our lot, no doubt when our mother wanted some peace. She kept a box of old broken china, from which we would be given a small piece to break up into minute fragments for the hens, in order to strengthen the eggshells. We loved doing this. There we would crouch in the hen-run, banging away happily, each with a small stone for a hammer, surrounded by a bevy of inquisitive hens, their beady eyes watching every move, ready to seize and peck whatever pieces were going. All the time they kept up a steady conversation of 'took-took-took' (hens really do have quite a vocabulary) while we would reply to them in their own language.

No record of early experiences with animals could possibly be complete without mention of cats. We always had cats; we always loved them – and they have enriched my life until the present day. Most of our family photographs from childhood show one or other of us hugging the cat. Cats tend to have bad publicity; they are generally seen as self-centred and lacking in affection. Nothing, in my own experience, could be further from the truth. A cat shown nothing but love and gentleness from kittenhood will respond with abiding devotion, although it will always have a mind of its own. One only has to look at the way in which a beloved family cat will allow itself to be treated by the children – being lifted, clutched round the middle and carted around with legs dangling, or dressed up and wheeled around in a doll's pram – to understand something of the gentleness of which it is capable.

Two of my earliest memories of sadness concern our cats. One was when Tigger, our handsome stripey, was lost for over a week and then came home, emaciated and in pain, dragging a trap on one of his legs. Although he eventually made a reasonable recovery, the incident left us with a hatred of all such instruments of torture. When I was about 12, the lovely black fluffy cat which was my constant companion, meeting me each day from school, went missing. For weeks I wandered disconsolately in the wood and the fields calling her name, but she never returned.

When a new kitten was being chosen, the gender was of prime importance, at least to our parents. Female cats in those days were perpetually producing kittens; the aim therefore was to choose a male. Sometimes, though, a mistake was made! Our cats, although 'house cats' in every respect, slept in a warmly-lined box in the shed. I shall always remember the sheer joy of kneeling there on the stone floor, gently caressing the tiny kittens as the mother cat fed them; she would always be purring as she did so, and she would wash each one with the utmost care. And as they began to grow, seeming to us like nothing more than little furry bags of milk, we discovered that even at that stage they too could purr!

Later, heartache was inevitable because unless we could very quickly find homes for the kittens (just occasionally we were allowed to keep one), we knew they would have to be drowned. This, sadly, was an inescapable fact in an area without a vet. I even recall the first time I heard that such a profession existed, when James Grant, a schoolboy who was a piano pupil of my mother's, announced his intention to become one – an ambition he duly realised. Doubtless one must have been called from somewhere from time to time – presumably from Inverness – for a sick horse or cow; certainly none was readily available for smaller animals, nor is it likely that many could have afforded such a service anyway. So kittens kept being born. We were, incidentally, perfectly aware of how kittens were born, but completely baffled as to why a cockerel was necessary if eggs were to produce chicks.

The demise of the kittens, then, led to even more tears than that of the pet hens. How we would have fared in the (necessarily) much harsher environment of a farm or croft is hard to say; probably we would simply have grown much tougher skins! For our tender-hearted father, to whose lot fell the unwelcome deed, it must have been a misery; he came from a family devoted to animals, each one of his brothers and sisters having beloved pets. Our mother, on the other hand, had been brought up to treat animals with kindness, but to regard their proper place as on the floor. It was left to Dad to compete with us to have the cat on his knee.

March was also the time for tadpoles. We would range far and wide with our friend Kathleen, armed with jam jars, until we found a satisfactory lump of the jelly-like spawn, and would bear it home in triumph. From then on the whole project must have been a nuisance for our mothers, who for one thing would be required to produce a suitable receptacle to house the growing tadpoles – not always easy in the pre-plastic age. Then there would be numerous expeditions to the river to procure 'pond weed' to feed them; we delighted in seeing rows and rows of the minute black creatures fastening on it, eating voraciously. Some years our tadpoles would be selected for nature study at school; this was a coveted honour. They would be carefully observed through each fascinating phase, the most exciting being when they acquired their legs. Seldom do I recall their actually reaching the frog stage; now it seems impossible to remember by what misfortune they met their end – perhaps we were somewhat less sensitive when it came to frogs?

While all of this activity was proceeding out-of-doors, a positive revolution would be taking place inside, for this was the time of the Spring Cleaning. Today, those of us who face up to this at all are likely to confront it in a fairly relaxed manner – a room a week, perhaps. Not so in those days! It was nothing less than a campaign, to be pursued relentlessly until everything, whether seen or unseen, had been dealt with (attacked may be a better word). Chimneys were swept; rugs, cushions, pillows and mattresses beaten; drawers and cupboards turned out and lined with fresh paper; doors and skirtings washed or painted; rooms papered or treated with distemper (the forerunner of emulsion paint); ornaments and china washed; pantry and larder scrubbed and disinfected; furniture and floors polished; silver and brasses burnished till they shone. And so it went on, day after day. In some ways Nan and I thoroughly disliked it, partly because meals tended to be irregular, but mainly because we were lazy, and did not appreciate having to help – by cleaning brasses, perhaps, or turning out our own cupboards and drawers. For once, we were glad to be sent to 'do our lessons'.

There were welcome aspects as well. For one thing, there was Greta, a girl in her twenties who lived on one of the highest crofts on the 'heights' behind us; for this one time of the year our mother had help with the blanket washing and general cleaning. We were fond of Greta and looked forward eagerly to her coming; she was cheerful and good-natured, even in the face of our non-stop questioning. Off she would go each evening, weary as she must have been, to face a mile or more of that demanding hill, always armed with two heavy bags of 'messages' (we never used the word shopping), which might well include a large can of paraffin for the lamps. Often since, having seen how invaluable rucksacks are to rural folk in Alpine areas, we have wondered why the bearing of burdens on the back did not find favour in earlier times with the Highlanders.

Everyone breathed sighs of relief when the battle was finally over. This was the bit we really enjoyed; there was a smell of sheer cleanliness in the house, indefinable, but compounded of something resembling bleach, furniture polish and fresh flowers. We would go happily from room to room, revelling in the freshness of it all – the crisp, starched curtains and bed-covers, the gleaming furniture; if our own bedroom had had the furniture re-arranged, that was a special bonus. Our father, always an inveterate tease, once startled our mother by suddenly saying 'You know, I'm afraid you've forgotten something this time!' Falling into his trap she anxiously asked what it was. 'I found a feather under one of the beds', he informed her.

The other good thing was that we were excused piano practice, the piano usually being under dustsheets at the time. It was a never-ending fight to get us to practise. To provide a much-needed boost to family funds our mother took occasional piano pupils; while she probably enjoyed some success with these, she had none at all with her daughters. We were both blessed with a keen musical ear, but this, alas, turned into something less than a blessing, for we immediately learned each piece by heart and simply would not learn to sight-read. In desperation after a fruitless couple of years she sent us to a 'proper' teacher in Inverness, our unfortunate father having to drive us there every Friday night. To no avail. We dreaded the visits, and were always badly prepared; after two more unavailing years we were abandoned as hopeless. We continued to enjoy playing by ear – the right hand correct, the left basic, as we never troubled to learn the chords. In later years we both took more happily to the guitar. In view of how much music meant to my parents, and the sacrifices – both of money and time – that they were prepared to make for us, it is a chapter of which I am now ashamed. Singing, though, has been a life-long joy.

One final event took place each year in March. This was the Scripture examination – the final one in the annual national curriculum of the Free Church; we would already, in November and January, have sat the Essay and Catechism exams. There were hundreds of entrants for these from all over Scotland, entering under various categories – junior, intermediate and senior. A gold medal was awarded for each age group, as well as several prizes, followed by first class, second class and merit certificates; we all dreaded being reduced to the lowest award! I believe today the standard would be considered exacting.

While altogether less formal and fearsome than the school exams, these were nevertheless taken seriously and prepared for assiduously. They took place, however, under the kindly eye of our minister and his wife, in the much less forbidding environment of the manse, where a prodigious amount of furniture rearrangement must have taken place before the entire flock of us were accommodated – not only around the large dining room table, but the study and other subsidiary tables as well. There would even be tea and buns to follow, along with much laughter – and sometimes exchanged fears if we knew we had not done well. But then we could forget about it all until June, when the *Instructor* came out; this was the national Free Church children's magazine, which would in that month carry pages and pages of results. It was exciting if, just occasionally, one or other of us managed to bring a coveted prize to the glen; but there could be humiliation as well, and we would vow to work harder next time.

This, then, was just another facet of the religious teaching we were all the time receiving; but there were other, less formal, ways in which we could not help absorbing valuable lessons, at times unconsciously. As the spring went on, it was as if some of the pastoral analogies of the New

Testament were brought to life around us. Take, for example, the parable of the sower; we might just be in the right place at the right time to see one of the local crofters sowing his corn by hand, in the age-old way. We were fascinated by this, and could readily understand the allusions to the various hazards through which valuable seeds could be lost – the predations of birds, the stony ground, the choking effect of weeds. Or we would see an ailing lamb being carried in the strong arms of the shepherd to be cared for, and would begin to understand something of the biblical concept of the Shepherd's individual care available for us. I remember too the sheer astonishment with which we realised that, although all sheep looked alike to us, the shepherd knew them as individuals!

We would have had closed minds indeed if we had failed to learn at least some of these lessons, for we were constantly being taught everything that was good.

APRIL

'PLEASE, MRS MACKINTOSH, could Nancy and Maisie come and see a mavis's nest?' In those days married women were invariably addressed – often even by their friends – by their full title; for a child to have used an adult's Christian name would have been considered the height of impertinence. The sole exception would be in the case of 'courtesy' aunts and uncles.

A mavis's nest! We had heard our friend Kathleen's polite request at the door and were swallowing our toast and marmalade at the double and were away out to greet her, clamouring to be off. Kathleen, a close friend with whom we shared many ploys, was the banker's daughter and lived very near, just on the other side of the hotel; of the many interests we held in common perhaps the chief was a shared obsession with bird-nesting. It would be no exaggeration to say that the finding and observation of nests occupied our minds to the exclusion of almost all else for the entire months of April and May.

Post-haste, then, we left with our friend, desperate to see the very first nest of the season. Thrushes' and blackbirds' nests were not difficult to find, and were referred to as 'ordinary' nests, but at the start of the season, anything was welcome. Kathleen led us quickly up the field to the wood – 'our' wood – and then along the side of a small burn almost choked with brambles, while we questioned her non-stop. 'Are you sure it's a mavis's? Is it lined with mud inside? Are there eggs? How many?' She just told us to wait and see. Then she stopped at the thickest clump of brambles and pointed. 'Over there!' We couldn't see it. 'Look again – over there!' And then, in triumph, 'April fools!'

Of course! How could we possibly have forgotten? Were it not that I

Nancy, Maisie, Jean and Kathleen, on Drumnadrochit bridge.

remember the incident as if it had been yesterday, I would seriously doubt whether we *ever* failed to remember the significance of April the first (even long before it became my wedding day). In the Highlands, much delight was always taken in practical jokes; an essential aspect, though, was that these must be accepted with good humour, so we laughed along with Kathleen at our stupidity.

Our childhood 'April fools' tended to be of the harmless kind, such as: 'Come and see this strange dog that's chasing our cat', or: 'Oh, look, Mrs Munro's parrot must have got out of its cage'. They seldom fooled anyone. Some older folk, on the other hand, could be quite ruthless; stories abounded of youngsters being sent quite long distances to buy tins of elbow grease or tartan paint. Worse, an unfortunate apprentice could be sent around the countryside bearing a sealed letter with the message 'Don't laugh, don't smile, send the fool another mile'. Like most children, we had a strong sense of justice and we felt this to be unfair; what chance did an apprentice stand of refusing to go anyway? Even hotels had to be on the watch for possible hoax bookings of lunches and dinners. As for us, we approved of pranks which were harmless but effective; one such was the placing of small mounds of earth as 'molehills' on the manicured lawn of an obsessively keen gardener. At 12 o'clock, mercifully, the season of hoaxes was over and all could relax again... until Hallowe'en.

The bird-nesting season, though, was only just beginning; we generally found our first nests in the first week of April. Soon it would be on in earnest! It would be the Easter holidays, when we would be free – apart from having to do some chores in house and garden, and within strictly laid-down limits – to roam the woods and peer into all the hedges, with Kathleen. She and Nan, both a couple of years older than myself, would undoubtedly have been happier without me trailing along behind. And trail behind I certainly did! They always seemed to be ahead of me, especially when it came to spotting a nest. 'I saw it too!' I would often wail, frustrated almost to tears when one of them would shout in triumph 'Look, a robin's!' just before I could get the words out. And they were completely out of my class when it came to diagnosing to which bird some strange nest belonged. Looking back, I marvel that they could have been so sure; perhaps Kathleen had a bird book, but we did not. Very occasionally our father would be called upon, if the nest seemed to be a game bird's – a snipe's or a pheasant's perhaps; he also taught us to recognise the nests of 'water-hens' (moor-hens) and mallards by the river.

As the season went on, there would be many highlights. Year after year, we steadily amassed more knowledge of nests and eggs, until even the hedge sparrows' nests with their exquisite sky-blue eggs began to seem a little tame, and we thirsted for more exotic finds – a pied woodpecker's in a hole in a tree, perhaps, or a meadow pipit's up on the moors, with its clutch of tiny chocolate-brown eggs. We became expert at raking a mossy ferny bank with our sharp eyes to spot the tell-tale curved edge of a yellowhammer's, robin's or willow warbler's nest, or, peering into a hedge, finding such gems as those of a bullfinch or a greenfinch. Sometimes, obligingly, the bird would fly out under our noses.

We definitely preferred well-made nests; finding eggs in a mere scrape with a few twigs by the riverside was all very well, but it did not compare with the thrill of seeing a 'proper' nest. Chaffinches, for example, were extremely common birds, but there was nothing remotely common about their nests, which were simply miracles of construction, coconut-shaped domes with mosses and lichen on the outside and lined with hundreds of feathers inside. Never, possibly, could we find enough of these! Wrens also built beautiful mossy nests, but they were less satisfying in that we couldn't see into them; if the hen bird was not in residence, we would gently reach our small fingers as far inside as they would go, to feel the warm smooth tops of the diminutive eggs. That was a special thrill, as was the sight of the tiny beady eyes of a robin looking out from its nest in a bank.

Once we even found what was obviously a cuckoo's egg in a hedge sparrow's tiny nest. We had been taught in our nature study class, of course, how the cuckoo will choose to lay its single egg in a small bird's nest; perhaps we had scarcely believed it to be true. Now we were seeing it for ourselves, and were faced with a moral dilemma. We were aware that the large cuckoo chick would proceed to oust the offspring of the foster parents; ought we not then to remove the cuckoo's egg? We held a solemn conclave. But we just couldn't bring ourselves to do the deed. Much later, returning to the nest, we found it absolutely filled by the large greedy cuckoo chick with gaping beak, and were guilt-ridden by our failure.

We must surely have lacked the collecting instinct, because we never removed an egg; on the contrary, we would mourn for an entire day if we found a nest that had been 'robbed' – either by humans or animals. Once, on a May weekend many years later, I remember telling a Glasgow colleague that two friends and I were going bird-nesting in their native Ayrshire. She looked at me in horror. 'Bird-nesting! But that's cruel!' It was my turn to be shocked. I hastily explained that we merely enjoyed finding and observing nests; afterwards, if the subject came up, I was careful to make this distinction.

All the same, it has to be said that it was principally the eggs that fascinated us. Later in the season, the nests we found would generally have young birds in them; when newly hatched, these would be naked, ugly little things, invariably with gaping beaks eternally ready for food. If there was a nest in our own hedge, we would try to count the number of times the over-worked parents fed their greedy nestlings, and would soon lose count. But while we found these baby birds decidedly unattractive (and always bewailed the fact that we had found the nest too late), it was an altogether different matter to come upon, say, a small flotilla of enchanting baby ducklings learning to swim on a pond, or, up on the moors, a family of young peewits, delightful balls of fluff, attempting to follow their parents on tiny uncertain legs.

Then there were our very own chicks to observe much nearer home. Great was the excitement when the allotted time of three weeks was up, and we would eagerly accompany our mother to visit our 'clocken' hen, to see whether there were any signs that the eggs were about to hatch. The one job we emphatically did not want to share in was that of lifting the hen off the eggs; usually she would squawk and peck quite ferociously. While she was held securely (backwards) under our mother's arm, we would peer at the eggs; sure enough, one or two would be beginning to crack, with tiny beaks peeping though. After that, each time we visited there would be more and more chicks. We were desperate to hold them, and eventually we would be allowed to. While the hen was being encouraged to eat some corn or mash, we would gently take one after another, dip its beak into a saucer of water, and wait while it daintily tilted back its head to swallow. When all had been helped to have a drink, we would scatter a mixture of oatmeal and water in fine crumbs, called *taois* (it is impossible to convey the pronunciation of this Gaelic word) and watch with delight as the fluffy chicks began to eat. Their mother would by now be clucking anxiously around them all the time, picking up crumbs in her beak and then dropping them again, to encourage them to copy her. The part we liked best was to see her finally settle back into her nest of straw, spreading her wings warmly over her cheeping flock. If one had been left behind, it was satisfying to see it scuttle back into the warm darkness beside the others.

Once again, a biblical passage with which we were very familiar was coming to life before our eyes; we had actually learned by heart the poignant words of Jesus 'How often would I have gathered your children together, as a hen doth gather her brood under her wings, and ye would not!' In all of this, it must be clear that we as country children had a distinct advantage over others who had never seen such things. It does not mean, however, that we were necessarily any more saintly!

Much later, though, would come the part of the process we did not enjoy at all. When the chicks were grown, to the extent of being able to fend for themselves, the netting run would be dismantled and mother and family released to rejoin the flock of hens. All would usually go reasonably well with the youngsters; the mother would be less fortunate, for she would – having by this time become a stranger – be attacked on all sides until eventually, after much suffering, she would be accepted back into the flock. Needless to say we suffered with her, shooing away her adversaries whenever we could. An even worse fate befell some fancy hens which our mother once attempted to import. They were of a breed called Barnvelders, greatly sought after at the time on account of their beautiful dark brown eggs; in those days the majority of eggs were white. The entire flock set upon them immediately; I clearly remember the pathetic sight of their combs, torn and bleeding profusely from quite ferocious pecking. I do not remember whether they survived or had to be given away. Hens can be extremely cruel and will on occasion peck a stranger to death.

Undoubtedly we saw hens in relation to humans and I have no doubt we learned some lessons from observing them so closely. For example, a small cluster of them 'took-tooking' in a corner would make us think of wifies gossiping. Again, there were high fliers that would insist on flying over the high fence into the garden; these tended to be of the Leghorn breed, wirily built and never chosen to be mothers. They would always have to be caught, to have their wings clipped. As for those hens which cruelly attacked others, happily we had never even heard of racism in those days – but it is every bit as ugly in fowls as in human beings.

If chickens tended to occupy our thoughts during the Easter holidays, so indeed did eggs, although it has to be said that these tended to be of the chocolate variety. At home, we were always given one small Easter egg each – cream-filled and with a 'yolk' inside – a gift which we prized and made to last as long as possible. Occasionally, visiting family friends would donate a much more exotic egg. On one memorable occasion, to our intense delight, we each received a large coloured cardboard egg, filled not only with tiny chocolate eggs but also with minute fluffy chicks. We kept those chicks for years.

Of the real Easter, as the great festival of the Christian Church, sadly we knew little, simply because it was not celebrated by the Free Church. It was not that we did not know the Biblical story; our deeply solemn observation of 'the Sacraments' strongly resembles the pattern of Holy Week as followed by many churches throughout the world. Although I now fully understand the thinking behind the Free Church stance, which is that the death and resurrection of Jesus Christ should not be limited to an arbitrary date in the calendar, and that Sunday should be regarded as a weekly celebration of the resurrection, I now feel this to have been a real lack in our young lives. To have been aware of sharing this supremely important festival with millions of fellow Christians worldwide, and particularly at that wonderful time in spring, which is surely redolent of the joy of resurrection, would have meant much to our young minds. In contrast, our Easter celebrations consisted of rolling our hard-boiled eggs down a slope and then eating them.

One of our great delights at the beginning of April was finding the very first primroses. If the snowdrop was our most longed-for garden flower, the primrose was undoubtedly our favourite wild one; we welcomed all the spring flowers – the celandines, wood sorrel, violets and wood anemones – but we *longed* for the first primroses. One Saturday at the beginning of April we were up in the wood with Kathleen looking for the first primroses; we found none. Moving up higher, we came to the fence separating us from a private wood always known as 'Miss Burgess's Wood'; this lady and her sisters lived in a small mansion house some way below. Sure enough, growing very near the fence was a clump of primroses. We simply had to have them! Slipping quickly through, we picked a tiny bunch, then made our way down to the main road near the hotel. At this point whom should we meet but Miss Burgess herself. She advanced upon us. 'Oh, aren't you clever girls!' she exclaimed. 'I've been up in the wood looking for the first primroses, and there wasn't one to be seen!' Absolutely tongue-tied, having no idea what to say, we stood silent. Very likely our red faces gave us away. Never again did we set foot in her wood!

By the end of the month the woods around us, and especially the banks overlooking Loch Ness, would be studded with myriads of primroses. In those days we thought nothing of picking huge bunches to take home in triumph to our mothers, burying our noses in them to drink in their fragrance again and again. A single bunch would fill an entire bowl; their scent would fill an entire room.

At some point in the Easter holidays we would usually be removed from the delights of the glen to spend a few days with our grandparents and aunt in the small town of Dingwall. This was a totally different world. Small town it may have been; to us it meant the ultimate in sophistication! For one thing, the house was bigger and grander than ours, and it had electric light and even, wonder of wonders, a vacuum cleaner – not that we coveted it, for it made a dreadful noise. Then there was the food; at home we invariably had porridge for breakfast, whereas here we were introduced to novelties such as cornflakes and grapefruit, the first we had ever tasted. The latter experience, I clearly recall, was somewhat marred because one of us got juice in her eye; we refused to touch grapefruit again for quite a long time.

Aunt Darla (her pet name from childhood) was always at pains to provide everything possible for our pleasure; she would find time to join in some of our games, and would sometimes take us for walks on the road alongside the Cromarty Firth – then a quiet road – in order to find and pick... primroses! What we really enjoyed, after we had overcome the challenge of it all, was to be sent for the messages. There were two highlights in this. One was a certain shop which absolutely fascinated us; it had a network of overhead cables by which the customer's money was sent to an office set high above the counters. From there, with a loud ring, a metal container would come clanking back along the wires with the change. We would plead with our aunt to buy things from that shop. The other was the greatest delight of all; we were sometimes given a penny to spend on ice cream – such riches! Not only did we *never* have ice cream at home (I doubt whether it even existed in the glen until much later) but Dingwall's Italian café owners, Morganti and Simonelli, made the best ice cream in the world. Ever since, I seem to have been searching for its equal! We would watch in absolute fascination as

The house in Dingwall (our grandparents' retirement home) where we spent our school holidays.

the girl carefully spread the delicious creamy concoction between two wafers to produce a penny 'slider'. Sometimes we were reduced to a half-penny cone, inferior but still delicious; whichever it was, we licked it as slowly as possible, making every drop count.

Another highlight of Dingwall holidays was a scooter that Aunt Darla had acquired somewhere for us. No sooner had we arrived than we were clamouring for it. The house had a paved pathway all the way round which was ideal for 'scooting', and we never tired of it. Once or twice we did get into trouble with Granda, a fanatical gardener, for dislodging pebbles from the sides of the paving on to his cherished lawn. All continued well, however, until one black year when we were told right at the beginning of our stay that there was to be no more scooter; some friend of our grandparents – possibly a doctor – had warned them that the use of a scooter, implying as it did much movement of one leg, was pernicious to growing children. In vain did we protest. The offending article had been placed well out of reach on the highest shelf in the garage, and we never had it again.

Our main argument, which cut no ice whatsoever, was that nobody was the least bit worried about hopscotch. This game – called 'beddies' in the glen – was a great standby in the days before children had access to much play equipment. Whenever spring came and the playground was dry, the craze for it would begin. All you needed was a flat stone and six squares drawn out on the ground or paving; you then kicked the stone, hopping continuously on one foot only, from square to square in a series of set patterns. Played as it was for hours on end, if anything was liable to over-develop the muscles of one leg, this was surely it! Yet nobody seemed to complain.

It is difficult to convey adequately to today's generation, accustomed to

In Dingwall with Aunt Darla.

multiple (and exotic) holidays, just how few and far between holidays tended to be back in the thirties. People on farms and crofts could not get away; many in any case could not afford 'paying' holidays. Apart from a few wealthier folk and those who had seen service in World War One, nobody had been abroad. There must have been many in the glen who had not travelled beyond Inverness, or who had had to be content with a day at the seaside at Nairn, the nearest coastal place. Most children would go at some time to stay with aunts and uncles or grandparents; some indeed would go 'on holiday' a mere few miles away, perhaps to the other end of the glen. We were considered fortunate in that we sometimes went for a week in summer (in addition to visits to relatives) either to Ullapool on the west coast or Nairn on the east.

We never went to the coast at Easter – with a single, regrettable exception which remains clear in memory to this day. That Easter visit to Nairn was, from the start, a dismal failure. The accommodation was spartan, the weather perishingly cold. To us, Nairn meant the beach; in days long before sea-life centres, wildlife parks, interpretation centres and cafeterias, if there was no beach there was little else to do. And on this occasion, although we had our pails and spades, we were frozen before we could even build a sandcastle. Still, I vividly remember the one great redeeming feature – to our intense delight, we discovered that Morganti and Simonelli had a branch in Nairn as well! Freezing cold the weather might be, but that didn't deter us in the least from enjoying to the full their delectable ice cream.

Because they happened so seldom, holidays in those less affluent days generated a degree of excitement and enthusiasm seldom experienced today. All the same, we were always glad to be going home, especially to see the cat again. And after the Easter holidays particularly, we could hardly wait for the first glimpse of the glen – a glen of almost unbelievable greenness.

MAY

W E ALWAYS washed our faces in the May dew. Despite being incorrigible sleepyheads – a failing which in my case has not gone away – Nan and I somehow never failed to be up at crack of dawn on the first of May. We did not dare to miss the early dew – reputed to be an invaluable aid to beauty; I was all too aware that this was a far greater necessity for me than for my decidedly more beautiful sister. I can clearly remember rushing outside to the clothes-drying green to gather up the dew in eager hands, washing my face, and then tearing inside to peer into the nearest mirror, hoping against hope for some miraculous transformation. Disappointment never seemed to stop me from trying again the following year.

The thrill of being out early on a May morning! – this is what remains most vividly in memory today. The glen in May (in retrospect, the weather was invariably warm and sunny) was little short of paradise. It was a feast for the senses, with exquisite colours and scents and sounds on every side. Perhaps even more than the rich colours of pansies and tulips and primulas, the *scents* of May-time entranced us; we would spend ages arguing about which was best, deciding first on lilac or violas (our favourite kind of pansy) and then moving on to wallflower. But in the end we always reached the same conclusion – nothing, simply nothing, could ever be better than lily-of-the-valley. Our mother had a lovely, delicate little vase with a sprig of lily-of-the-valley painted on it; this was brought out each year to be filled with the fragrant flowers whose scent spread through the room. That time seemed to signal for me – and indeed still does – 'the height of the year', the perfection of May.

As for sounds, I admit that we were surprisingly deficient in the realm of birdsong. It is hard to say just why this was. The commoner songs, of course, we knew well, such as those of the robin, mavis and blackbird; hearing the cuckoo and the lark was a thrill repeated each year (there were many more larks in those days). From our garden, too, we frequently heard the drumming of a woodpecker (the greater spotted; we knew of no other) in the wood above. And, like all country dwellers, we knew and loved the plaintive call of the curlew – there can surely be few more beautiful or evocative sounds on earth. One call we most certainly did not appreciate was the craking of the corncrake, which, if the field behind us was under corn, could go on and on at night until we could cheerfully have shot the bird; that is a thing of the past now.

There were some songs of which we knew nothing; it was to be many years before my keen bird-watching husband introduced me, for example, to the richness of the songs of the willow warbler (we called it willow wren) and its cousins the wood warbler and garden warbler. I cannot say, either, whether I ever recognised the amazing volume of sound produced by the tiny wren; even the well-known 'little-bit-of-bread-and-no-cheese' of the yellowhammer was not familiar to me, although this colourful bird (and its nest) certainly was.

It was, all the same, the 'feel' of May-time, the sum total of all these delights, that made us at times almost intoxicated with its beauty. I can recall racing up the field to the wood above and sitting under one special birch tree on a cushion of greenest moss, looking around at all the primroses, violets, wood sorrel and 'wooden enemies', and feeling almost ready to burst with the joy of it all – thinking at times, too, that I couldn't possibly bear ever having to leave the glen.

Interestingly, I have found *air maduinn Cheit* (on a May morning) to be a recurrent phrase in those Gaelic songs in which praise of the beauties of nature is poured out; many Gaels in the past must surely have loved this most lovely of months.

It is perhaps this intimate 'feel' of the seasons that is the most difficult thing to convey to those unfamiliar with the countryside – the feel of a windy day in March; of a breathless, hot day in August; of a golden day in October – each with all the sights and scents and sounds thrown in. It was precisely this which, years later in the city, seemed hardest of all to bear – the awareness that the precious months and seasons were passing, with little other than man-made events to punctuate them.

Less seriously, though, it was an altogether different kind of feeling that tended to be uppermost in our minds during those early May days –

and that was the hated prickly warmth of the long black stockings we had been obliged to wear all winter and spring! We would be desperate to get them off. 'Mam, when can we start wearing our short socks?' we would plead again and again. We always called our mothers 'mam'; in our slow glen drawl this came out rather like 'ma'am' – arguably, more dignified than today's more matey 'mum'. And then again 'Mam, when are we getting our sandals?'

Just what a relief and joy it was to be allowed to change into summer clothes is almost impossible to explain. One of the (few) things I envy today's children are their light-weight, comfortable clothes, so easy to wear; sweatshirts, quilted anoraks and elasticated skirts and trousers would have delighted us! As it was, our clothes always seemed to be too tight, too hot, too prickly, too baggy or too fussy; we were always 'growing into' garments bought (for frugality) too big for us, or else growing out of them; our 'best' dresses had bows, belts, ribbons or frills and were often a nuisance. Once, when cycling home in the dusk, I collided with a bat, which became entangled in the large bow at the neck of my blouse; extracting it was a nightmare experience. When we complained, we were told in no uncertain terms to be thankful to have good warm clothes to wear, as so many lacked them.

Despite the generally-held opinion of older folk that one should on no account 'cast a clout before May was out', I believe we did usually succeed in persuading our mother to allow us to dispense with at least some of our cold weather garments. This might mean merely wearing a blouse instead of a thick jumper under our gym tunics, but even that was truly welcome; changing to short socks and sandals, or a cotton dress, was nothing short of bliss. First, though, there had to be a visit to Tavish's shop.

Tavish MacMillan was a well-known character, highly respected in the community and the United Free Church, of which he was an elder. He kept a shop in the village of Milton, which meant a walk of about a mile for us with our mother. I remember it as a draper's, a shoe shop, and much else besides; what I remember most clearly, though, is the special smell of the shop – probably mostly of leather, for he kept what seemed to us a vast stock of shoes, boots and wellingtons, as well as clothes. He would patiently bring down shoe-box after shoe-box from the highest shelves, all the time carrying on a conversation with our mother, until finally we were fitted with brown leather sandals (for best wear) and brown or black canvas 'sandshoes' (for running around) – the latter being, I suppose, the thirties' equivalent of trainers – except that they were cheap! We all wore them; they would, needless to say, be bought slightly too big but might well end the summer with our toes beginning to poke through.

All the time that Tavish spent wrapping the purchase meticulously in brown paper and string (as all who ran a shop in the days before plastic bags were able to do to perfection) we would be champing at the bit to be away, to get home and try the new shoes on again and perhaps, just perhaps, talk our mother into allowing us to start wearing them.

This particular visit prior to summer was regarded as a great treat. Getting new clothes generated much excitement because it happened so rarely; our mother generally made (or had made by a dressmaker, who occasionally would stay with us for a couple of days while she sewed) our dresses and blouses. Jumpers, cardigans, scarves and gloves were home-knitted except when sometimes received as Christmas presents. Actually going to a shop to buy something new was something of an occasion.

Later in the year there would probably be another visit to Tavish's shop, but although we liked him and enjoyed going, this (pre-winter) one was nothing like as popular, as it meant the purchase of our warm vests, knickers and 'liberty bodices' (to hold up the hated long stockings) and, worst of all, 'combinations'. To any child allergic to wool, these must have meant absolute torment; we simply disliked them heartily for being hot, prickly and desperately uncomfortable.

Such then was our relief when early summer arrived. For our mother too there was one particular cause for relief when the light evenings came, bringing to an end the one and only chore I ever remember her, a keen housewife, complaining about – the cleaning of the lamps. There would always be a whole row of these, ranging from the large ones, like the Tilley or Coleman pressure lamps and the Aladdin, which gave a softer light, through the small ones for the bedrooms, to the tiny lamps for the bathroom and hallway. All had to be cleaned and filled with paraffin; their wicks had to be trimmed, and at times replaced; a new mantle might have to be fitted to the pressure lamps. In all, it was a smelly and tedious chore. Sadly my mother never lived to see electric light come to the glen.

One anecdote concerning the lamps I heard her tell so often that I cannot now be sure whether I actually witnessed it or not. My sister had very long thick hair which was brushed very thoroughly morning and night. One evening when my mother was busily engaged in brushing, Nan, aged about nine at the time, did something we had both been warned never to do – she held the comb over the lamp, where it immediately caught fire. Coolly she turned and threw the blazing comb unerringly into the fire. Lamps were always potentially dangerous; the flammable nightdresses of the time could cause tragic accidents.

It was in May, with 'the yellow on the broom', that the tinkers would come. We did not call them 'travellers' in those days. Looking back, I seem to recall in us as children a somewhat ambivalent attitude to them; we were just a little afraid of them, not because of anything they did but because they represented something strange and alien to our settled mode of life. It was strange, for example, to see children in those days wearing earrings, or a woman smoking a clay pipe. But we also felt sorry for them having no fixed abode – totally unaware at the time of how greatly they valued their free way of life and how little they would have appreciated our pity! We felt sorry for the children having to come to the doors begging with their mothers, for the skinny horses that had to draw their heavily-laden carts, piled high with women and children and belongings, and for the even skinnier whippet dogs that invariably ran alongside tethered to the carts. It would be fair, I think, to say that in a sense their coming somehow disturbed us.

What remains most vividly in my memory is my mother's attitude to the tinkers. Observing her closely as we always did, we could not but notice her kindness and patience, and marvel at it. A woman with perhaps a couple of children in tow would arrive at the doorstep and, almost before the door was opened, pour out the contents of her suitcase. We *knew* that, whether Mam needed anything or not, she would find something to buy – some clothes pegs perhaps, or a potscrubber, or a card of safety pins. 'Never send anyone away empty,' she would always tell us (and the teaching stuck, for I have never done so... except for once, when I was inordinately busy, and I felt so miserably guilty that I sent my unfortunate husband out later to find the doorstep salesman!)

Then the requests would begin. Did my mother have any clothes for the bairns? Of course she did; out would come a couple of our outgrown jumpers or skirts. Had she by any chance a drop of soup? Yes, she had, along with some bread or scones, or maybe a pot of jam; I even saw her produce a bottle of cough medicine or cod liver oil for an ailing child. And so it would go on, until in a firm voice my mother would say 'Sorry, no more today,' and without any argument the woman would gather up her belongings and depart, not without many blessings and warm expressions of thanks. It would be easy to take a cynical view of these; I believe myself they were entirely genuine. And when some of the tinkers returned soon after my mother had died – tragically, while still not past middle age – they broke our hearts by talking sadly over and over again of 'the kind lady who never turned us away'.

She treated tramps in the same way – so much so that our father would often tease her that one day he'd be left without a shirt for his back. A single amusing exception, which our mother often told as a joke, comes to mind. One day a tramp had sent her back and forward with such an unending string of requests (and never a word of thanks) that even she lost patience and retorted 'That's enough now; you're just a humbug'. Whereupon he turned and marched towards the gate, muttering in time to his steps: 'Humbug, humbug, humbug...' One of the tramps who came year after year intrigued her on account of his extremely cultured accent, but she never did learn his story.

Another incident, totally unrelated, also comes to mind. Years later – I would have been in my twenties – I went on holiday to Poolewe in Wester Ross with my Aunt Darla, my mother's younger sister. As we walked through the village one day I noticed a cartload of tinkers approaching, and then suddenly, to my complete astonishment, we were literally surrounded by smiling brown faces, as hands were stretched out from all around. Not to me, though! 'Miss MacKenzie!' they were greeting my aunt, and shaking her hand with the utmost warmth; 'Good to see you! How are you keeping?' So it went on for several minutes, while she in turn enquired about various members of the clan; finally they moved off, with many blessings and expressions of goodwill. The explanation had to be dragged out of her, but it appeared that for several years, when they were encamped near her home, she had been helping them to fill in necessary forms, and writing letters for those who were illiterate; she also read the Bible to them on Sunday afternoons. As a family we were well aware of what a special person she was; clearly, though, we were not alone in this assessment.

Our mother had given up her work as a 'pupil teacher' in a small Ross-shire school when she was married. She was, I believe, a born teacher, and in a sense she never did give up – she taught us all the time. Unlike our father, who was easy-going (and whom I never remember demanding anything of us at any time) she could be very strict, and there were undoubtedly times when we would have longed for the more relaxed attitude of some other children's mothers. But she was just, and above all she was kind. She taught us 'good manners' – not just the cultural conventions, such as how to behave at table, but the more important underlying courtesy and thoughtfulness for others.

She taught us, for example, always to take some gift, however small, when we went on a visit to receive hospitality. Not just any gift, either, but an appropriate one planned with some care. Needless to say she taught by example; we saw her give gifts of fresh eggs, home baking and preserves; cut flowers and home-grown vegetables were superfluous for country dwellers, but suitable for friends in the town. To someone who was poor – and in those days there were many – she would take perhaps half a pound of tea, or for an old person living alone, a pot of nourishing soup. During the war, when everything was scarce, it might be something baked with precious rations. These were unforgettable lessons.

She taught us – *how* she taught us! – to write thank you letters. Woe betide us if we should dare to write merely 'thank you for the present'. We had to name it and say exactly why it was so very acceptable – and if we couldn't say this with total honesty, we had to emphasise the kindness and thoughtfulness of the giver.

Our mother also taught us something which seems to be dying out in today's society – to say something was our fault, and to say we were sorry. I believe we learned through this the truth of the Biblical text: 'a soft answer turneth away wrath', for it was simply the case that after we had confessed and shown contrition, the whole situation was mended. Even so we didn't always do it!

One thing she dinned into us was to be polite at all times. It had never occurred to me for a moment to wonder about the wisdom of this teaching, until a well-known personality, also from a Highland background, wrote something like this: 'We were brought up to be so polite that I believe we would have had no idea how to react to assault; we didn't know how to scream'. That, I think, could well have been written of us. We were blessed in those days more than we knew, living such a safe and sheltered life; not all, even at that time, might have been as secure as we were, although I feel sure – certainly in rural areas – most would have been. But faced with any kind of assault, would the deeply-ingrained sense of having to be polite to our elders under all circumstances have actually been dangerous? Thankfully we did not have to find out.

Our very favourite and most exciting wood springs to mind, known locally as 'the cover' (probably more correctly *covert*) to which we begged to be allowed to go from early spring onwards. It was exciting for three reasons: there were to be found in it many garden flowers growing wild, first snowdrops, and later daffodils and narcissi; it was a wonderful place for birds' nests; and in places it was so dense that you could easily get

The glen looking towards Loch Ness showing the 'cover'.

lost. Despite this, I don't recall ever feeling afraid in it. At one place there was a big pile of stones where we believed a weasel lived, and we had been told that weasels sucked people's blood. This was our sole fear! As for our mothers (I mean ours and Kathleen's, for we always went together) I very much doubt whether they ever feared for us. It has to be said that we invariably got a row on our return, because we never failed to be late, but this was simply for missing homework, or because one of us would have filthy shoes after falling into a bog. It was never, I believe, because they had been worried.

The cover would be at its brilliant best in May. Not only would there be huge clumps of primroses and pheasant-eyed narcissi, but the marshy places would be aflame with golden marsh marigolds; in the latter part of the month wild hyacinths (bluebells) would cover the wood like a carpet. The trees too would be beautiful. It was a mixed woodland of birch, rowan, ash and elder, wonderful flowering cherries (geans), and alders by the banks of the river – they like to have their feet in the water! The white 'candles' would be out on the horse chestnuts, the white blossom in all its spring glory on the geans. All in all, it was to us a veritable fairyland.

On those May visits we would be having a second – or even third or fourth – look at all the nests we had found in April; they would generally belong to small birds, but occasionally we would come across the nests of pheasants, moorhens or snipe. Indeed there was no telling just what exciting nest we might find; on one occasion at least it was a sandpiper's on the shingle by the river. The 'cover' ran down both sides of the river, all the way to Loch Ness, about a mile in all. I shall never forget the strange sensation as we reached there for the very first time and stood, overcome with awe, looking at the dark shining waters of the loch and realising we could go no further. I am sure we felt something like David Livingstone and Christopher Columbus rolled into one.

In the tamer part of the glen, what comes to mind most vividly is the immense amount of cultivation there was in those days in comparison with today; sadly, in many areas of Scotland a ploughed field has come to be something of a rarity. In May, with the ploughing, harrowing, rolling and sowing well past, there would be a great deal of new growth everywhere.

There would always be a great many potatoes, that trusty standby of Highland people for generation after generation. In many fields around us too, the young corn would be bright green. 'Corn' is, of course, the generic term for the predominant cereal in any area; in our case it was certainly oats. The vital part played by oatmeal in Scotland through the centuries makes a fascinating story; it was a great deal more than a food, being a kind of currency as well – a unit of rent, and part of the stipend of both ministers and schoolmasters. In the thirties it was no longer still used in all of these ways, but it was important in the diet – so much so that it would have been difficult to imagine life without it. It was always recognised as a most nourishing food. What could possibly be better than porridge with cream, oatcakes with butter, or leek and potato soup made deliciously creamy with oatmeal?

All the same, I confess that our hearts used to sink when rotations decreed that 'our' field should be ploughed, harrowed and sown with oats, for this meant that we would be restricted to a narrow path round the edge on our frequent excursions up to the wood. The only others to regret it even more than us were the hens; their little door into the field would be closed off, and they would be left with just the hen-run which, although reasonably large, could not compete with the expanse of field in which they normally scratched happily. We noticed, incidentally, that they tended to be more cantankerous with each other when so confined. From time to time in frustration one or another hardy spirit would contrive to fly over the high fence, and would lead us a merry dance until recaptured.

Often in late May we would enjoy a spell of glorious warm weather, some memories of which remain clearly in my memory – one from earliest schooldays and one from just before their end. I have already tried to indicate the extent to which our school was – excessively, as we firmly believed – geared to constant work rather than to play; in the early summer, however, there would at times be a barely discernible relaxation of the customary stringency. When we were in the lowest classes, one rare treat was to be taken out on what was known as a 'ramble'. We always longed for these but would never have dared to ask for one; indeed, to my best recollection we were never allowed to ask for anything, except – in dire necessity – to leave the room.

After the teacher had announced the imminent ramble, excitement would run high; we knew better, though, than to express any of this aloud, and soon a very orderly crocodile would leave the school and make its way up the side road to cross the main Great Glen road and follow the sandy track leading to Balmacaan House, the local mansion. The estate was spacious, heavily-wooded and criss-crossed with many well-maintained paths. Thereafter we would stop numerous times to be shown some of the wayside flowers – wood sorrel, coltsfoot, speedwell, tormentil, birdsfoot trefoil – and to learn the names of the commoner trees. By this time there would usually be a slight relaxation of the 'no talking' school rules to permit someone to draw attention to anything especially interesting. It could be an owl's pellet, some type of fungus, perhaps an insect or a butterfly; occasionally something really earth-shattering would cause a child to shout out, for example: 'Look, Miss, a squirrel!' Otherwise, all would be conducted with great decorum; we knew well that this was our best chance of another such treat. To be fair, it must have

Hugh A. Fraser, headmaster, with some of the school staff, a few years before our time.

been quite a responsibility for a teacher to have charge of two fairly large classes on those occasions.

The second memory is of a very different time – a rare afternoon off, when my best friend Joan and I had finished our Highers and were within a few weeks of leaving school. Making his preparations for departure at the end of term was our headmaster, Hugh A. Fraser MA, after more than 20 years in office. In those days, when schools had minimal secretarial assistance and Information Technology wasn't even a faint cloud on the horizon, the two of us had been chosen to help him to clear out a pile of official papers and, among other things, to produce a graph of school attendance over his reign, and a roll of dux prize-winners. We had often seen him at his most irate – which was fearsome, to say the least; now we met him at his most human, kindly and courteous. He treated us like ladies, and even had his housekeeper bring us tea each afternoon on a silver tray! Our self-importance knew no bounds.

One beautiful afternoon in late May, after we had completed our allotted tasks, he generously allowed us to go home very early – a thing almost unheard of in our school. With our mothers' permission we set off to walk up to the heights to the north of the glen, beginning with our own familiar wood, and then on past several crofts.

At one particular place we had a quiet chuckle as we recalled an anecdote from many years back, which had been relayed to my mother by the mother of a boy in our class (on whom I, and at least two others, had had a crush all through primary school). The house in which his family had previously lived, and which we were now passing, had a strong fence round it, beyond which a path led to a series of steep outcrops, potentially dangerous for young children. Not surprisingly, he had been strictly forbidden ever to go through that fence. One day when he was four, his mother found him on the banned side of the fence. 'What are you doing there?' she roared at him. 'A hen pushed me,' he meekly replied. This handy phrase has been used in our family for years, whenever one or other of us is aware of offering a totally unacceptable excuse for some misdemeanour.

Having passed all the dwellings, we went much further until we reached the start of the wild part – the heathery moors, which stretched for miles behind the cultivated face of the glen. Eventually we found ourselves following the course of a sizeable burn; reaching a beautiful pool fed by a small waterfall, we couldn't resist removing shoes and socks to paddle in the brown peaty water. Afterwards we sat, munching our sandwiches in perfect contentment, allowing the warm sun to dry our feet.

In perfect contentment? In a sense, of course, I do recall it as such. But

I also remember some mixed emotions. There was certainly a strong feeling of freedom and of enjoyment of the place; inevitably, too, there was a sense of excitement at being at last grown up, on the threshold of a new phase of life – even to have come this far, much farther than we had ever reached before, and with the moors beyond beckoning...

Yet there was a shadow at the back of my mind. In only three months, student life in the city would be beginning; what would that be like? Did I really want to go? I forget now whether I shared those doubts with Joan, although there was little we were not accustomed to discussing with each other. It was still wartime; I have no recollection, though, of any sense of fear in exchanging the safety of the glen for potential danger in the city. Nor was there, at the time, any sense of regret at leaving home; there was too much eagerness to be free of parental control for that. If I had known that in just two short years the first real shadow was to fall, and I would be summoned to the doctor's surgery to be told that my mother had inoperable cancer, how different that would have been!

No, the cloud on that day had to do with one thing only – this beautiful glen that I would have to leave all too soon. How on earth, I wondered, could such a thing even be contemplated? Having left, we would of course return often. But would things ever really be the same again?

JUNE

'MAM, WE met Peggy and she's asked us up for Friday night – please, please, can we go?' A visit to Peggy's! There were few things we liked better. We would plead; we would promise faithfully to do all our weekend lessons, even our piano practice, on Saturday when we returned. And of course, in the end, we would be allowed to go to Peggy's.

I suppose we went only a few times, maybe once a year during our early teens, but those visits made a profound impression. They could well have taken place at any time of the year (except the dead of winter), but I like to think of them as having been in June, when the ditches would be full of fox-gloves, ferns, pignuts and budding meadowsweet, and the glen vegetation was beginning to be overgrown as the days drew on towards midsummer.

Peggy was, even in those days – when she would have been thirty-something – a 'character'. Our mother, although fond of her, was never entirely comfortable with her because she tended to be excitable; she also had a disconcerting habit of looking you straight in the eye and saying 'Can I ask you something?' As this would invariably be something personal, such as which boy in your class you were most keen on, you would begin to blush before she had even put the question; what was most maddening was that you still blushed even if the name she then suggested was that of someone you couldn't stand! Despite all the teasing (a very popular form of humour in the Highlands), we thought the world of Peggy. She was the youngest of a large brood; sadly none of her brothers had been keen to carry on the family croft, and – as frequently happened in those days – she was the sister left at home to look after her elderly father.

To get to Dalreach you first had to go about three miles 'west the glen' by the main road (I cannot now recall whether we went by bus or on our bikes) and then up the hill for another winding mile-and-a-bit, passing one farm and several cottages and ending up in a beautiful wild area of scrub birch and juniper. We loved the place, with its feel of remoteness. Whenever we went, there would be so much to savour on the way that we always trailed up very slowly. I can see Peggy now, buxom arms akimbo and a huge smile on her face, coming down to the last gate to meet us and demanding 'What on earth kept you?' Nan and I would be there with our close friends Joan and Rena; Peggy was really their friend rather than ours, a frequent visitor at their home, the Free Church manse, but she had kindly adopted us as well.

I find difficulty in remembering the house as it then was because of its later refurbishment into a modern letting house. Probably it was at that time a standard family croft house; what I recall best is the open fire from which a black pot or kettle hung on a 'swey'. As for the menu, it was never in doubt; Peggy knew our fondness for hard-boiled eggs and cheese sauce, and that was what we had each time. Never had we seen so many eggs cooked at once! She was always known as a generous provider, not only then, but in later life when she became a celebrated B&B landlady, to whom guests came from literally all over the world.

Soon we would be sitting down to prodigious helpings, but not before Peggy's father had pronounced a lengthy blessing on the food, arguably even longer than our own grandfather's. Nan and I often used to feel it

Achtemrack – next to Dalreach, Peggy's house. Sadly, there is no picture of Peggy herself.

would be better to say grace *before* the food was served, to save it from growing cold. After supper there would be some work to do; quite rightly, one never got away from Peggy's without joining in whatever had to be done, for her life was busy; it might be anything from helping to stack logs or peats to bringing in kindlings or weeding a plot. After that, though, the fun would begin. What the old man thought is not recorded, as shouts of laughter would echo from upstairs; somehow nights at Peggy's always ended in hilarity. We would perhaps be trying on old outfits of hers, or being allowed to wear her high-heeled shoes – how we longed to have these for our own! We would persuade her to parade in one of her smart suits – she dressed extremely well 'for best' – generally favouring dark brown or black, which suited her figure and her beautiful red-gold hair. Then there would be 'the books' (family worship) taken by her father, before we finally went to bed in the tent-like coom-ceiled (sloping-roofed) rooms. Sleep would not be long in coming, after the excited chatter had ceased.

In the morning there would be quite a ceremony, I remember, over the porridge. Old Mr MacKenzie would be sitting eating his when we came downstairs; he would have a cup of creamy milk beside his bowl of porridge, into which he would dip his spoon with each mouthful. This, apparently, was the proper, traditional way to eat it, the idea being that in this way the milk was kept cool and the porridge hot. Not until we had copied him and finished ours did we receive our second course – another egg. Soon we had to say our farewells and make our way down the brae towards home and our weekend's homework.

Dear Peggy – it hurts now to remember her, always the centre of a laughing, talking group, because of the final years when a stroke so cruelly deprived her of speech. And yet those were happy times, and it is surely good to remember.

If February was the month for snowdrops and April for primroses, June was the month for roses. The wild ones – dog-roses we called them – were in one respect disappointing; although they looked so lovely in their colours of white, pale pink and deep pink, they had no scent, and scent in roses was what we were primarily interested in. Some of the old-fashioned 'moss roses' we had in our gardens in those days had wonderful fragrance. But there was, above all, one place where Nan and I could be sure of finding roses with a quite incomparable scent, and that was halfway up the hill to Drumbuie Farm, where we were often sent on a Saturday morning for the milk. They were small, pale yellow roses, and there were hundreds of them, growing wild over a fence nowhere near a garden, but surely at one time having been cultivated. Whatever their origin, they absolutely entranced us, and we could scarcely tear ourselves away from them, burying our noses in their fragrance over and over again.

In those far-off days before milk bottles, we had a large tin milk-pail with a wire handle. Into this Miss Tolmie, the farmer's sister, would pour a generous three pints of creamy milk, which we loved to see frothing into the pail; there would often be an apple or a sweetie for us as well. Although this milk would of course be perfectly fresh when received, one cannot help wondering just how well it would have fared by the time it reached home with us – first, because we loved to swing the pail (knowing exactly how far we could swing it without spilling), and secondly because we took such an unconscionably long time to complete the journey (about half a mile along the road and then another quarter up the farm track). There would always be so much to see and do! There would be gates to swing on, cats to stroke, stones to kick along the road; according to season, there might be wild rasps or brambles to eat, oak apples or acorns to gather from beneath the tall oaks, a foal or calf to admire in the field, nests to look for... On one famous occasion, Nan poked a wasps' nest in a bank with a stick; she ran away fast and I didn't, and I was stung four times.

In June our father would go fishing on Loch Ness. Normally this was not his scene at all; he was *par excellence* a trout fisherman, a fisher of the hill lochs, from which he would, with ease, bring back a basket of gleaming brown trout in a single brief evening. Loch Ness was different – 'a stiff brute of a loch', as it was often called by the angling fraternity. Nor did Dad have enough spare time to make the effort worthwhile. He might be engaged in painting a fence or building a shed, digging the garden or sawing logs, and it cost 30 shillings to buy a licence for a month – a fair sum in those days. I don't know that he ever really enjoyed it either; all one had to do was to troll some kind of metal minnow behind the boat, a process involving none of the precise casting at which he was so adept. But it was a chance to catch a salmon – and a *single* salmon (which could be big) was usually all that he did catch. Some fishers would come from afar, fish the loch all day and land a number of salmon; they would then pack them in special long boxes and send them post-haste to London for sale. Dad despised all such commercialism; his fish would be divided up into generous pieces and given away to friends who, like us, would enjoy one or two delectable meals.

Nan and I would always pester him to take us out in the boat – an elderly rowing boat, which was kept in a kind of backwater of Urquhart

Maisie rowing across the bay to Urquhart Castle.

Bay, at Temple Pier. We would occasionally be given our wish on a calm evening, and might even be allowed to take over the tiller of the *Seagull* outboard motor for a short spell; as we got older, we were also taught to row. Normally we would have a very brief trip across the bay to Urquhart Castle and back. But one expedition, when Dad ventured to take us much further, ended ignominiously. We were trolling fairly close to the shore parallel to the Inverness road, and had covered perhaps a couple of miles, when a sudden squall came up; big waves started to rock the boat violently, and water came in as fast as we could bail. Nan and I became very scared and began to cry, with the result that our father was forced to beach the boat and leave it, and then hitch a lift for the three of us back to the car. Hopefully he got some peace after that episode; I remember that we were none too keen to risk the dark waters of Loch Ness for some time!

It was in June that the local Mod took place each year. These festivals of Gaelic music are popular today, attracting competitors young and old to various venues around Scotland. Our local one was the Lochaber Mod held at Fort William, some 50 miles distant. Let it not be imagined even for a moment, however, that we, the pupils of Glenurquhart School, would be allowed to enter – it would of course have hindered our school work! It was to be several years before some of us did actually take part. But for many weeks before, we would return from school to hear our mother at the piano, singing one of the songs she was engaged in

Glenurquhart Gaelic Choir in the late 1930s. Our mother is in the centre of the second row.

learning for the competitions. At least once – for I still have her award – she was the competitor with the highest aggregate of marks. Then there was the Glenurquhart Gaelic Choir, of which she was an enthusiastic member. On one memorable occasion the Shield – the premier award for choral singing – was proudly displayed in the window of the grocer's shop in Drumnadrochit.

The Gaelic language – today both adults and children clamour to learn it; tiny children can even be introduced to it through Gaelic playgroups. How sadly different it was in our childhood, when not a word of it was heard in our school; even the songs we sang in class were translations into English. And yet at the time, probably all glen natives over the age of 35 spoke it!

It has always been to me a matter of profound regret that we missed learning Gaelic as children, and by such a short head. If, say, we had been brought up on one of the high crofts, or perhaps a few miles further up the glen, or if both our parents had been Gaelic speakers (Dad understood plenty, but did not speak the language) how different it might have been! As it was, my friend Joan and I did make an attempt to learn it in our early teens, going for 'conversational Gaelic' to an elderly gentleman, Mr Dan Gollan, who was a fluent speaker. Alas, we were already learning French and Latin by the bookish method then in vogue; we simply could not learn without understanding grammar and spelling. The single thing that somehow remains in my memory is the Lord's prayer in Gaelic.

We were, all the same, brought up with much more than a smattering of the language; our speech was peppered with Gaelic words for which we scarcely knew the English equivalent. We would be sent, for example, to 'put a *rian* on our room' (tidy it); one of us might have, not a fringe but a *dosan*; a chicken was either male, a *coileach*, or female, an *eireag*, and so on for a great many words and expressions. It was to be many years before, frustrated by this hotch-potch of half-knowledge, I finally made the effort to pull it all together and study for an 'O' Grade; when I began to apply myself, I sometimes felt that the language had been lying asleep inside me, waiting to be brought to life. This was true, at least, of the pronunciation, which seemed to come naturally. Admittedly the grammar was something else altogether! Sadly, despite having acquired the ability to read and write to a certain standard, I know I shall never *speak* Gaelic; in even attempting to follow the news, I am left at least three items behind.

When we were children, we were acutely conscious of our lack of know-ledge on the fairly rare occasions when we were allowed to attend Gaelic concerts. We would sit there uncomprehending as the *fear an taighe* (chairman) would let loose a positive flood of Gaelic; it used to seem that he was deliberately telling one joke after another, while those who understood made a special point of rocking with laughter. This offended us greatly! We felt very much excluded, especially as, deep down, we were convinced that we were in fact every bit as truly Highland as those who had had the good fortune to be brought up speaking the language.

Why then was Gaelic not more prevalent during our childhood? Why did parents not make a point of passing it on? As I see it, although to some extent that cultural ethos still prevailed which had deliberately and cruelly repressed the language and culture of the Gaels (my maternal grandfather growing up in Wester Ross would, if caught speaking a word of Gaelic at school, have a thread tied tightly round his ear for the rest of the day) there were other reasons as well. It was partly the fault of the parents themselves, in that they tended to reserve Gaelic for matters they did not wish their children to share; this we knew well from our own grandparents, and very maddening it was! In addition there certainly existed the attitude that you shouldn't waste your time with Gaelic if you wanted to 'get on' in life. Sad, but true. Presumably it was this that precluded the teaching of the language – which was our rightful heritage – in our school.

This need to study, to 'get on', was dinned into us all the time, and by and large I suppose we accepted it. Certainly I have no memory of questioning such views – until one day years later when, making my way home from Canada, I was paying a brief visit to New York. At the request of an elderly lady who had been a close friend of my mother's, I called on her brother there; he had left the glen as a young man, and had prospered in business in the city. He kindly took me out to a very smart restaurant, introducing me to the head waiter in his acquired Yankee accent as 'a girl from my home town'; he had never married, and this was where he had all his meals. As I left him that evening, I couldn't help comparing his lot with that of some of his former school-mates after whom he had been enquiring, and who had spent their lives in the glen. No doubt he enjoyed city life; but what I had seen was a lonely old man. Still, he had 'got on'... hadn't he?

On two occasions – the Silver Jubilee of King George V and Queen Mary in 1935, and the Coronation of King George VI and Queen Elizabeth in 1937 – we were actually given a day off school, to be treated to a varied programme; in both cases there was a service followed by speeches, a picnic and sports, with, at night, a bonfire on the neighbouring hill. My memory of these events is hazy (nor do I have any idea of what became of the medal and commemorative mug, which I know we received) but what I do remember, for the simple reason that they were so unusual, are the sports.

There were some pupils whom I recall as having been outstanding at sport; probably it would be more accurate to say potentially outstanding, for they were given none of the help and encouragement they would receive today. Emphatically, our own group of girls were not of their number! One year one of our fathers went so far as to set up a rope for us to practise high jump; we were of course totally hampered by our skirts, but even tucking them into our knickers made little difference – we were simply pathetic! Could we have been all that feeble at running too, I wonder? Certainly on one famous occasion when a bull chased us (or at least we thought it was going to) I seem to remember covering the ground pretty fast. The only 'race' at which I excelled was the 'tortoise cycle race' – something we practised informally many times – and if anyone imagines it is easy to stay on a bicycle moving in centimetres, they should try it sometime! I have often wished we had been brought up on skis in the same way that we were on our bikes – even cycling 'no hands' was easy meat to us in those days.

Much more enjoyable, though, and considerably more relaxed, were the races held during our Sunday School picnic, usually held on a Saturday in June. Those I remember best took place at the ruins of Urquhart Castle on the shores of Loch Ness – visited today by a quarter of a million Nessie-hungry tourists each year, but in those days generally quiet. The

Urquhart Castle, scene of Sunday School picnics.

races were run in a section of the wide grassy moat of the castle; they were mainly fun races – egg and spoon, obstacle and the three-legged race, at which Joan and I excelled, for the simple reason that after much practice we were able to run with abandon, almost forgetting that our two inner legs were tied together.

Afterwards we would prowl around the ruins (the dungeon was always a favourite place, despite the fact that it gave us the creeps) using our imagination to recreate the past, as well as using it to delude ourselves that from the tower we could see large ripples made by the monster. At tea-time, an invariable feature of any children's 'treat' was the handing out of 'baggies' – paper bags, one for each, containing an assortment of buns and cakes. In our day, these were a treat for the simple reason that they were *not* baked by our mothers; we habitually had scones, pancakes and shortbread, all home-baked, but to have baker's delicacies, especially if they were iced, was wonderful! The final, and extremely noisy, part of the tradition was that you blew up your baggie and burst it.

The year I was 10 remains in my memory as truly momentous. Just occasionally in a lifetime, something can happen which at the time may seem like quite an ordinary event, but in retrospect is seen to have had immense significance. So it was when I was 10, and following a vacancy in the Free Church, the Matheson family came to the glen. Is it merely imagination, I wonder, or do I truly remember the day our father told us of their arrival? However that may be, I know our first eager question concerned the age of the children. This was always the vital thing to be established whenever a new girl appeared in our class – not simply her age, but her birth date. In the Mathesons' case we had to wait a day or two; then, to our delight, we learned that their three girls' ages encompassed our own, the order being: Maimie, Nan, Rena, myself, Joan. And Joan was in my class! Their brother, Ewan, was a few years younger.

It did not take long for a close friendship to develop – which included, naturally, our friend Kathleen – and soon much of our free time after lessons and chores was spent at the manse.

Joan Matheson – my best friend from age 10.

It was perhaps unfortunate for their mother that the whole group of us tended to play at their house; hospitable to a fault, though, she never seemed to mind. The glebe was large; their front garden had a substantial area of rhododendrons and other shrubs and trees, ideal for hide-and-seek or the game which soon became our passion – kick-the-can. I can still so easily recapture the excitement of those games when, heart pounding, one would manage to sneak out of some perfect hidey-hole to kick away the can and 'save' the game.

The manse family had lots of animals – a cat, a dog, a family of particularly omnivorous goats, a large flock of hens; the new minister was also a keen beekeeper. All the same, what they really specialised in was people; over the years we were to have the privilege of observing the motley collection of folk who beat a path to their hospitable door – old friends, new friends, people in need of one kind or another, tinkers,

Mrs Matheson.

tramps, even at times the hopelessly drunk. Nobody was ever turned away. One of my most abiding memories – and the scene was a recurrent one – is of Mrs Matheson baking scones at one end of the table in their ample, 'heart-of-the-house' kitchen, while at the other end her scholarly husband would be peacefully immersed in some Hebrew text or theological tome.

Let it not be thought, then, that theirs was any theoretical exposition of the Christian faith; day in, day out, they simply lived it. And on that day when they first came to the glen, how little did I imagine that a life-long, deep friendship was beginning, which would in a very real sense change the direction of my life. At first, what it meant was mainly the joy of having a best friend; although fortunately never bullied at school (the worst I endured was being called skinny – which today would be a compliment indeed) I was to find how infinitely better it was to enjoy things, learn things, share things and laugh at things with a special friend, with whom I was to go through the whole of school and even, later, share the same profession. Apart from this, though, there was to be so much more in the future. How could I have guessed that, in all too few years, Mrs Matheson would become a second mother to me when my own dear mother died, or that, over the years, I would be warmly welcomed into a second home there again and again, or that the manse would become a place of solace for my father when he was eventually left alone?

One final, poignant memory will suffice. It is of a day years later, when my own life had reached a low point. My parents were dead, Nan was married in Canada, I was recovering from the only serious illness I have ever had, and my old home was probably to be sold. For some reason, Mrs

Matheson, along with Joan's newly-wed husband (also a Free Church minister) had come with me to see to things in the house. I remember standing there looking round at my childhood home – the house empty, the garden over-grown, the hen-run bare except for nettles. Suddenly grief took hold of me, and I cried as I had never cried before, for all that was lost. And these two held on to me and, I believe, wept with me. They must have known – indeed they did know – how far I had by then wandered from the old ways, and that my life was in a mess through alcohol. What they silently offered

Revd Farquhar Matheson.

me was a totally accepting Christian love. It is a day I can never forget; and I believe that small but significant event marked the beginning of a new and better path for me.

The second of the 'Sacrament Holidays' and another season of Communions took place in June. As in February, devout folk from near and far would flock to the glen to take part, probably in greater numbers because it was summer. From the time Nan and I became 'extras' in the manse family, we became more aware of all that this entailed for them, simply through finding ourselves in the thick of the action! We might be in the kitchen when parishioners brought in produce – anything from potatoes and vegetables to butter, eggs or cheese, or a leg of lamb, or a trifle. All of it was required! All kinds of visitors would converge on the manse, and the amount of hospitality dispensed would be simply prodigious.

Instead of all the services being taken by the local minister, according to Free Church custom at least two ministers from other areas would be invited to come; they would of course stay in the manse. In addition, other (often uninvited) guests might appear, perhaps just for a meal but possibly also requiring a bed.

As habitual visitors to the manse, Nan and I were certainly not about to miss any of this highly interesting activity if we could help it! We would beg to be allowed to go, and in answer to our mother's inevitable misgivings would promise faithfully that we would 'help' – and we might indeed assist with some minor task, such as dishwashing.

As quasi-family members, we would frequently find ourselves included in the augmented family worship, generally led by the visiting minister in residence at the time. As the assembled company would usually 'read round' – one verse each of the scripture passage – we would feverishly scan the portion ahead to identify our own verse, anxious to be able to read fluently. It should be stressed that we did take this act of worship seriously; simply because of nervous tension, though, there was always a

The Matheson family (left, Mr Matheson with Rena and Ewan; right, Mrs Matheson with Joan on her lap and a friend and Maimie behind).

lurking fear that one of us might start to giggle, for example if our verse should happen to include an unpronounceable Biblical name.

Little did the visiting minister in charge realise just how keenly his appearance, his accent and his slightest mannerisms were being observed by the six children there! That mistakes could be made in our assessment of him was as true in this case as in many another hasty estimate. Mrs Matheson herself (who knew the perpetrators in her youth) often told us a particular tale. In a certain Highland manse the visiting minister, well known for being unusually long-winded, one evening unexpectedly ended his prayer so promptly that the two young sons of the manse were surprised, when the kneeling circle rose, standing on their heads in the middle of the floor!

On the Thursday, the 'Fast Day', the services would be of the normal type. Friday was completely different, for at the morning service 'The Men' – so called simply because they were not ministers – were required to 'preach to a text', being given (to my knowledge) no advance notice of what this might be. The service could be extremely long, but even as children we could become drawn into the atmosphere of intense devotion, often amazed at the fluency and passion of the men's preaching. As church elders and lay preachers, some might well be unlettered men, but outstandingly gifted preachers, easily able to hold a congregation spellbound. To those who were not able to do this, the ones who stumbled, our hearts would go out in sympathy.

Sunday morning was obviously the culmination. It is difficult to imagine a more solemn or reverent occasion; indeed it is impossible to convey adequately to those unfamiliar with the background the intensity with which the Gospel would be preached; often, several of the congregation would be in tears. The church would be packed, a number of the earlier Gaelic congregation having stayed on, for their Communion Table would be served before the English one. The old church had been built to seat well over a thousand, but was accidentally burned down in the fifties and replaced by a much smaller one.

For me, part of the moving atmosphere derived from the Gaelic singing. Often, on an ordinary Sunday morning, we would be standing outside the church waiting to go in while the final psalm of the preceding Gaelic service was being sung inside; the clear voice of Duncan Fraser the precentor would be heard, rising flute-like as he 'gave out the line', to be followed by communal singing full of the ancient 'grace notes' – each singer being free to add personal improvisation. The combined sound is dissonant, and very strange to many listeners, but it has its own beauty;

as a child, I used to think that nothing could ever sound as reverent. Interestingly, in recent years I have come to love Gregorian chant, which seems to share this note of extreme reverence and humility.

When the time came for communion, people would walk slowly forward to the singing of some verse from Psalm 118. The part which most gripped my attention was verse 19:

O set you open unto me
The gates of righteousness;
Then will I enter into them,
And I the Lord will bless.

It would seem as if those walking forward were actually passing through some kind of awesome, shining gates. They would then sit round the Table, with its snowy cloth, with bent heads. Sometimes the minister, as if expecting somebody who should be there, would say: 'Yet there is room', and one who had for some reason been holding back would slowly come forward to join the others. There would follow a lengthy prayer; then clinking sounds would be heard as the elders went round collecting the 'tokens' before the bread and wine were dispensed.

After the lengthy service, the large crowd of visitors would somehow be absorbed by the local congregation, and invited home for a hearty meal. Nan and I particularly enjoyed this, especially the excitement of not knowing who they might be. Many would return for the evening service. Then on the Monday a service of thanksgiving would complete the 'communion season'.

One thing did, it has to be said, mar the occasion for us as children. This was the fact that our own parents were not communicant members. This was not unusual. While our father had not been brought up in the Free Church, our mother most certainly had; her father, an elder of the old school, had so instilled into her mind the 'wrongness' of singing at concerts and *ceilidhs* that she felt unable to go forward for membership. How sad this always seemed to us! We knew her deep faith; did she not constantly share it with us? Young as we were, we knew that she sang with beauty and dignity the songs of our people. Could there be anything wrong with that? We found it hard to understand – even though we were all aware that the previous Free Church minister had been strongly censured by some for belonging to the local Gaelic choir. We had of course heard tales, from an earlier century, of new converts burning their fiddles or breaking their bagpipes – tales which never failed to cause our hearts to sink.

Perhaps our mother lived too soon. Later, she would have seen attitudes soften, as people came to see the wonderful diversity of our different cultures as something precious given by a God of infinite creativity, to be treasured and held in stewardship just as surely as the beautiful natural world – although never to be accorded the central place in life. Yet there would be much to sadden her in today's culture; without doubt, she would have repudiated the idea held by some that the ethnic life of the Gael can be recreated through the language and culture alone, without regard to the essential spiritual dimension.

I have often been asked about the effect of these sacramental occasions on us as children. Did we ever feel repressed? At times we did; the general ethos of the day could be decidedly repressive. We could be not only inspired and elated, but also awe-struck and frightened. Some of the ministers – and even more so, 'the men' – had an aura of blackness, or at least bleakness, which centred on doom and judgement and seemed to lack that essential joy that the Gospel, meaning, after all, 'good news', should surely bring.

As always, though, one strives for total honesty and balance, and many of us would say we are grateful to have been taught the seriousness of the human condition. Some might also claim that today the pendulum has swung too far the other way, and certain forms of worship are little more than entertainment. It is also worth noting that children are remarkably perceptive; we were drawn, not to the excessively pious and forbidding, but to those men and women who seemed to us to have the most loving spirit. Those were the ones from whom joy appeared to flow, often allied to a rare sense of fun. They are the ones we tend to remember.

It seems to me now that there was at the time a preoccupation with what would now be termed 'micro-ethics', questions of whether it was right, for example, to use a car on Sundays, to go to 'the pictures', or – and this was the one that generated most heat – whether a woman should ever use lipstick (or even powder) or have her hair permed. Such things came under the heading of 'worldliness'; it seems to me now that less concern was expressed over more serious faults, such as gossiping, greed, quarrels, and lack of forgiveness. The more liberal faction were delighted at one time to receive an unexpected boost from a highly-respected Free Church professor who, when asked the question in a debate: 'Is it right for a woman to put on her face what God did not put there?' replied, quick as a flash: 'Is it right for a man to take off his face what God did put there?'

Other things did happen in the year I was 10 – things unusually materialistic in an altogether unmaterialistic lifestyle. Our Uncle Jimmy, Dad's oldest brother, died very suddenly while still comparatively young. This was the first family bereavement Nan and I had known, and it was a sad time; we were very fond of him – even though we dreaded having to listen to him playing his bagpipes indoors! He was a piper of some repute; his obituary notice in the *Ross-shire Journal* has it that 'he excelled as a teacher of pipe music, some of his pupils taking foremost places in piping competitions at various gatherings throughout the Highlands'. He was also a popular adjudicator at the Strathpeffer Highland Games.

Uncle Jimmy left our father a legacy of several thousand pounds. The exact sum is not known to me, but what I do know is that, on the glen grapevine, it became grossly exaggerated! All the same it was, for the time, a significant amount, and inevitably made quite a difference to our lives.

The first thing that happened was that we acquired a car. True, it was only a modest Ford, but it was brand new! The sheer excitement of this – still, in the thirties, something of an event in the glen – is not difficult to recall even now; we were beside ourselves with impatience waiting for it to arrive. One day Dad came home and told us (he should have known better) that Alex Menzies, proprietor of the garage in nearby Lewiston, had just promised he would be given three days notice of delivery. From that day on, we would give him no peace. Each day, we would shout 'three days notice?' the minute he appeared home; and one day, the great news did at last come that the car had been delivered. Away we went post-haste to fetch it from the garage. Alas! A two-door model had been despatched instead of a four-door, and our disappointment knew no bounds. To cheer us up, Dad asked if we might at least sit in the 'wrong' car. I can still recall the smell of the new leather, and recapture the thrill of that day. Our own car arrived a week later.

Trips in the car quickly became part of our lives – with visits to our grandparents in Dingwall or to Inverness sometimes on Saturdays, and to our friends up the glen, our horizons began to broaden. Much as we appreciated the new dimension, though, we had to confess, more or less guiltily, that travelling in a 'closed' car failed to be quite as exciting as our very first motor trip a couple of years earlier. One day a Mr and Mrs Peebles, friends of our parents from Edinburgh, had arrived in an open car with the hood down; it also boasted a 'dicky' seat at the back – something like an open boot but with a seat, on which we were allowed to sit with our mother. We were then taken for a run along Loch Ness-side to Invermoriston, about 12 miles distant. What a thrill it all was! We bowled along, the wind blowing our hair over our faces, totally unable to hear each other except by shouting. We were, I remember, most reluctant to get out of the car at the end; nothing quite so exciting had ever happened to us, and it was hard to sleep that night. Each holiday season after that we used to hope against hope that the couple would come to visit us again, but they never did.

Petrol rationing hit us hard, needless to say, when the war came. For many months the car would have to go unlicensed and would sit, dead and useless, in the garage. Then Dad, frustrated, would decide to put it back on the road again, perhaps just for a spell of three months.

At one such time, a bizarre incident occurred. We had gone to visit our grandparents in Dingwall one winter Friday night and, returning the long way round via Inverness (our mother having been afraid of possible ice on the dreaded Beauly Brae), we were making our way slowly along the road by Loch Ness – and I mean slowly and with the utmost care, for the lights, when permitted, could have been measured in candle power. It was late, and Nan and I were both asleep in the back. Suddenly a crash jerked us awake; before the horrified gaze of all four of us, a horse, which had been standing in the middle of the road and which had reared up so that its front hooves had crashed down on the car's bonnet, trotted away into the blackness. As it went, our parents could faintly make out a dark shape falling from its back. Quaking, poor Dad got out to investigate; quaking we sat inside awaiting his report. Great was our relief to hear that the horse appeared quite unhurt, the object that had fallen was a large sack of straw, and the owner – a well-known habitual drunk – was sleeping peacefully in a ditch nearby. The car, unfortunately, was *not* entirely unhurt, but it did get us home safely. I have always regretted losing the brilliant drawing of the incident which Donnie MacKintosh, a boy in my class, produced after word had got around.

The next consequence of our new-found affluence was that we acquired a radio. A 'wireless set' in those days was quite a handsome piece of furniture, and ours, a 'Cossor', was no exception. The snag, though, was that it had to run on batteries – a 'wet' one which had to be charged approximately once a week, and which was a constant trial to our father, and a 'dry' one, which lasted several months. Its use was meticulously rationed, certainly as far as we were concerned; it was primarily reserved for the news, or occasional programmes of Gaelic singing (there was great excitement when our mother was recorded on one of these) or Scottish dance music. In later years, the two programmes I recall best were *Monday Night at Eight* – the first variety show we ever heard – and the ever-popular *MacFlannels*. One altogether more sinister memory is of hearing Hitler's voice and the answering roar of the Nuremberg crowds; although we were too young to understand much of the Nazi menace, I remember quite clearly how it frightened us.

One more thing that happened in that eventful year – or maybe it was the following spring – was having an extension built to our bungalow; this consisted of a large roomy kitchen in place of the small 'kitchenette', as well as an extra WC and washbasin in the back part of the house. Nan and I were absolutely fascinated by each stage of the building process – the floor, the windows, the plumbing, the plastering – and must surely have been a nuisance to the tradesmen with our incessant questions. We had never before seen building in progress, new houses being something of a rarity at the time. Later, we were also able to 'supervise' a garage and a flight of concrete steps as they were being built.

It was all quite exciting, of course; but as far as I can remember we never did give any real thought to houses, either our own or those of our friends. The only thing I remember is that after having spent holidays at our grandparents' house, we would think how good it would be to have stairs! We were aware that our house was comfortable and pleasant, but I really believe that the spacious garden, the field behind, the wood and the nearby river meant more to us.

It was in Canada, where I lived for a couple of years in my twenties, that these considerations were brought to my notice for the first time; there, there seemed to be great emphasis on houses. What kind of house did I live in in Scotland? The question took me by surprise; I remember having to think before replying. What did houses cost there? I hadn't the slightest idea – nor yet about refrigerators (practically nobody had one), nor wall-to-wall carpets (I had scarcely ever seen one), nor 'matching drapes' (almost all our curtains were very old indeed).

It set me thinking. I thought of some of the humble cottages in which many of our closest friends lived; even then it was hard to be sure whether they even had a carpet (except in the best room), or was it perhaps just a home-made rug in front of the fire? What I did know was that they had a *real* fire, and the welcome was warm!

That was in the mid-fifties. In the glen the age of materialism, of consumerism run riot, had not yet begun.

JULY

FROM ABOUT the end of May onwards, we lived for the summer holidays. First, though, there must take place the biggest event in the entire school year – Closing Day. At no other time, not even at Christmas or New Year, was there such a scene of frantic activity – exhibitions of school work to have finishing touches added to them; class songs to be practised till each pupil was word – and note-perfect; pieces of sewing laboriously completed and ironed to a high degree by the mothers; pieces of knitting sewn up and, again, pressed to perfection by the mothers. The girls' dresses would be as full of ribbons and frills as could possibly be achieved, and ironed to the most immaculate standard imaginable by – yes! – the mothers again.

The scene so readily returns to mind; we would go home at lunchtime to find the whole kitchen redolent of that special ironing smell (hot beeswax on the old flat-irons) and see our own best dresses hung up carefully on hangers, while our freshly laundered petticoats, and even handkerchiefs, would be laid out on the bed ready for the great occasion, along with our white socks and polished shoes. The boys did not get quite the same treatment; they were scrubbed and polished, brushed and combed so as to be almost unrecognisable, but were still not the birds of paradise we were.

We would swallow our lunch and be helped into our finery, and then, in high excitement, be away back to school at the double, to be marched in a class crocodile up to the public hall. This was quite a splendid building – certainly for a rural area like ours – and had been gifted by a benefactor, Mr Bradley Martin, around the turn of the century. It stood, conveniently, just a few minutes' walk from the school, and was used on

Blairbeg Hall, where the school prize-giving took place.

all the grand occasions. Class by class, we would file in, excitement kept well in check, and sit quietly waiting until the back part of the hall filled up with parents, grandparents and interested locals, and finally the platform party moved in; this would consist of local dignitaries, including perhaps the ministers, the doctor, the headmaster and some important personage who would make a speech.

The opening part of the afternoon's programme would be a kind of concert, beginning with the youngest classes and working up to the combined senior choir; during their performance the conductor (the headmaster) would at some point walk away to leave the choir singing in perfect time without his help – a piece of pure showmanship. Some of the individual items must surely have been boring in the extreme for the audience (although, in those unsophisticated days, I doubt if people used that word). A single personal example will suffice: I once had to recite the entire 10 *double* verses of *The Relief of Lucknow*. More acceptably, there might well be sung duets or quartets; once Nan's class performed a playlet on the classic theme of the lady of the manor running away with a gypsy. Nan was the lady and sang a solo, wearing – to my intense envy – a long dress. All the music, incidentally, was vocal in those days; the selection of musical instruments available to schools today would have made us envious indeed.

Next came the speeches; if memory is correct, a short report on the school year by the headmaster, followed by a longer one from some invited speaker. At long last it would be time for the prize-giving. This part I do recall clearly – the sitting on the edge of one's seat as, class by class, the time came for our turn. It was of course exciting to win a prize, and yet our attitude was necessarily ambivalent; while one would be assured of approval at home, and it was the least our mother expected, this was not so at school – it just didn't do to be seen as a swot! As for the prizes we did win, we would often wonder, somewhat unkindly, who on earth had chosen them. They would almost always be boys' books; if they weren't, they were about girls at boarding schools – an alien world to us. One title I still remember, although I no longer have the book, was *Lyn Hayward, Slacker*; we had to read the book to find out what a slacker was! For a brief period in our early teens, we wished we could go to such a school; most of the time, though, we were firmly of the opinion that life was a great deal preferable where we were.

The excitement of Closing Day would last for hours after we had gone home. We would, for example, take time to look at our personal contributions to the displays of work, and would find them quite impressive! Remembering the many times we had dropped stitches in our knitted socks, or had had to take out stitches in our sewing because they were not neat enough, recalling how desperately grubby the entire piece had become, we would marvel at the way our mother's finishing touches had miraculously transformed the garments.

After this it was goodbye to school. In those days, eight whole weeks would stretch blissfully, and seeming endlessly, before us, for school closed in the first week of July and did not recommence till the first week of September, although I believe the other holidays were correspondingly shorter. Away would go our finery until the next party; meanwhile we would change into our oldest clothes and our sandshoes, and be away up to the wood or down to the river.

Next morning brought a different perspective. Holiday time it might be, but the initial part, we knew, meant some quite hard work for us – probably the most sustained effort required of us in the entire year. It was up to us to pick the blackcurrants! This may seem unexceptional, but in our garden there were perhaps a dozen bushes hanging with pounds and pounds of fruit, all waiting for our attention; this fruit formed a very important part of our winter food.

We would begin the work in fine form, each with a large receptacle and a stool to sit on; naturally we would compete with each other to be the first to fill the bowl and receive our mead of praise. By about the third afternoon, enthusiasm would have begun to wane; our mother would then have to begin sugaring the pill by giving us, perhaps, more alluring duties in between, like feeding the hens or going to the shop. Still later, we would have a couple of hours off to go and play with friends. But we knew there was a great deal of fruit to be picked; neither parent had the time, and it was simply up to us. Also, it had to be done properly; we must 'pick clean'. This meant two different things; each bush must be completely cleared of fruit, and the currants themselves must be 'clean', with not the tiniest trace of stalk left on.

What we failed to appreciate, needless to say, was the vast amount of work those pounds and pounds of fruit meant for our mother. As with the marmalade, preserving it was not a matter of producing a few pots, but rows and rows of two-pound jars and more than one large crock, enough to last, at the very least, until the following spring. In those days, while the vitamins were still being discovered, and before ordinary folk were aware of the very high vitamin C content of blackcurrants, housewives still knew the value of giving hot blackcurrant drinks in the winter, especially if someone had a cold.

Blackcurrants might have been the most important – and labour-intensive – crop, but there was plenty of other fruit to be dealt with as well; there were raspberries, strawberries, redcurrants and gooseberries, which would either be turned into jams and jellies, made into puddings, or eaten fresh with cream. What an undreamed of joy a freezer would have been to our overworked mother in summer! Later, probably during the war, bottling fruit in kilner jars came into fashion and our mother became adept at this process; all the same, it was nothing if not labour intensive.

Crawling under the net to pick the strawberries was not a task we relished, and it tended to be left to our ever good-natured father; when birds had sometimes to be cut out of the net after becoming hopelessly entangled, though, we learned to mend the holes. The rasps stood inside a high enclosure and picking them was more desirable work. I still remember two special canes which produced yellow rasps with a sweet honeyed taste; there was always competition for these. The gooseberries, though prickly, were not difficult to deal with; when they had reached the stage of being really ripe, fat and yellow, they burst deliciously in one's mouth.

When, at last, the bulk of the fruit had been picked – and bulk is certainly what I mean – we really began to enjoy the freedom of the holidays. There would still be duties to do in the mornings, such as weeding, or dusting our room, but afterwards several options were open to us. When we were small, a favourite treat was to have Kathleen along to tea. 'Tea' properly speaking, would be real tea with scones and biscuits on a tray at the top of the garden, where our father had built a most attractive arbour with rustic woodwork, around the trunk of what must have been a very large tree; this made an excellent table. But the real attraction would come later. We would have our doll's teaset out, and on each of the tiny plates would put some garden fruits. We would then have a pretend tea-party, always a most genteel affair conducted in what we believed to be 'ladies' voices'. 'Do have a meringue', we would urge each other, or 'try my cream sponge', as we passed a plate of redcurrants. We would play like this happily for hours; strangely, though, I cannot recall ever actually playing with dolls.

When we were older, to be allowed to play down at the river with our friends was considered best of all. The Enerick, although to be greatly feared in some seasons, would usually have shrunk in summer to a fairly shallow stream with numerous pools, in which there lived many tiny fish; armed with jam jars, we would 'fish' for hours for these. Fortunately we had soon learned that it was useless to try to keep them; despite our attempts to feed them with a selection of weeds, they would always be dead the next morning. The chase, therefore, was all; having caught them, we were resigned to letting them go.

There is an amusing sequel to this. Many years later, I took my son Kenneth, then aged about 10, to the river and taught him how to catch these fish, which he knew as minnows. 'No, not minnows', I corrected him, 'these are called *spreeds*'. He wondered why we should call them such a strange name. 'It was a glen word', I assured him, 'everyone called them spreeds'. He was doubtful. As it happened, we had a caravan at the time which stood near the house of an elderly lady known locally, because of the work her father had done many years before, as 'Jeannie the Carrier'. Although rather deaf, she had an excellent memory and we loved hearing her talk about the old days. 'When you were children,' we asked her one evening, 'did you ever fish for those tiny fish in the river?' Yes, of course they did. 'What did you call them?' I asked. 'We called them spreeds,' she replied with confidence. 'I think it was a glen word'. Ken was impressed! From then on, he was content to catch spreeds as well.

Needless to say, we were not allowed to wade across the river; sometimes, though, we simply could not resist the temptation. It wasn't that the other side was any more attractive; there were the same trees, the same flowers – ragged robin, meadowsweet, campion, marsh marigolds – the same spreeds in the pools. I suppose it seemed more exciting simply because it was forbidden. Once, indeed, it was a shade too exciting altogether, for as we reached the opposite bank a bull looked at us from behind some wild rose bushes! We splashed back to our own side faster than we had ever done before. Crossing the river was in any case far from enjoyable; there were jagged stones covered with slime, and there could be broken glass. Almost every time we disobeyed orders and waded across, it seemed, something would happen to give us away. Usually it was one of us falling in; even if we managed to dry out wet garments, the crushable materials of the day would refuse to look normal. When accused, we would always confess – I hope it is the truth to say we always did tell the truth! On one occasion I went home expecting great sympathy from my normally sympathetic mother when I had cut a toe badly; I did not get it.

It would be around this time each year that what we were pleased to call 'the circus' would arrive; we would be going to the post office perhaps, and there it would be – several caravans and side-shows, spread around Drumnadrochit green. What we would be most excited about, I remember, were the swing-boats; no matter how often one of us would be sick after sampling their delights (and on at least one occasion it was certainly me) we would be more than willing to try them again.

When Nan and I were in our early teens, Dad taught us to shoot – at a target set up in the field, never at an animal – with a .22 rifle; we were therefore eager to show off our prowess at the 'shooting' stall. I recall occasionally winning a cheap ashtray or glass dish, but just once, much more usefully, not one but two cycle repair outfits! Nan, incidentally, later became a competent shot and a member of the Aberdeen University team.

The highlight of the circus, though, would be a kind of gymnastic performance by a young girl dressed in satin and sequins; the sole item that remains indelibly in memory would be announced with a loud fanfare as 'the double twist of the body!', whereupon she would bend over backwards to pick up a handkerchief in her teeth. We thought this wonderful (and vainly attempted to emulate her). Alas, after we had all visited Bertram Mills' Circus when it came to Inverness one year, all was changed; we had seen much greater things, and had become sophisticates! All was not lost, however; I believe it is true to say that most of us pitied the animals in the 'real' circus and were relieved that our local, lowly one did not include these. On the whole, we continued to enjoy the novelty of it when it came.

Another excitement of the summer was weddings – there was simply nothing Nan and I loved more than a wedding. Living next door to the local hotel was a huge bonus. We had only to hear the sound of the bagpipes to stop whatever we were doing (especially picking fruit) to run inside for two chairs; perched upon these, we had a grandstand view of the hotel garden, where the happy couple and their guests would be piped around a lovely pond surrounded with trees. It pains me to record that this self-same pond is today inhabited by a huge plastic monster – the kind of 'monstrosity' that commercialism has inflicted upon our beautiful village.

Afterwards, we would eagerly pick up any pieces of confetti we could find, especially the tiny silver-paper bells, which we hoarded for years. One year, bringing added excitement, there was the wedding of Auntie Hal, Dad's younger sister, in Inverness; we prized, and kept in a special box, the dainty 'favours' from her wedding cake.

All the same, I believe the obsession with brides (for it was only the brides we had eyes for) went back to a certain period of several weeks when both we and our close friends the Mathesons were at home in quarantine while suffering first from measles and later from chickenpox. Apart from the initial fever and spots, I recall that time as truly pleasurable. At some point we were given paper cut-outs and scrap-books; of these, it was a series of brides that captured our attention. Thereafter – despite our general lack of artistic ability – we painstakingly learned to draw 'ladies' faces and outfits, specializing in brides, of course. Later I recall having got into trouble at school for covering the back of my jotter with these drawings.

It was not until we had reached our teens that we were allowed, during the long holidays, to go for trips of any length on our bicycles, despite the fact that the roads were unbelievably quiet in comparison with today's. I remember how we used to envy the members of numerous cycling clubs who used to pass, wave after wave of them, during the weeks of summer; they would wave and shout to us as we stood watching from the garden.

The very first time Joan and I were allowed to go for a 'real' cycle run remains clear in memory. It was to Invermoriston, a scattered community by Loch Ness, some 12 miles south-west of our glen. The day was fine, we were in the highest of spirits over our adventure, and in no time we had covered the miles and were approaching Invermoriston. It was time to choose a picnic site; we found a beautiful place in a clearing (I still notice it in passing today) where we lit a fire and boiled our picnic kettle – good smokey tea made our sandwiches taste so much better! It goes without saying that making tea in this way is infinitely more satisfying than having it tamely from a thermos flask.

Afterwards, I recall, we visited a girl in our class who lived near there; pupils from all along the loch-side as far as Fort Augustus came by bus to our school – always causing us much envy because they were allowed out earlier than we were. Of another trip, this time to Inverness (14 miles) I remember much less, perhaps because on that occasion there was no picnic. I do know that it afforded great satisfaction that the bus fare was saved, and the extra cash could be spent in the Rendez-vous Café in town.

July, for us, normally meant holidays spent at home; it was in August that we had a holiday away. But one July, when I was 11, there occurred a truly memorable exception; we went to Edinburgh. This would mean little today, but if one bears in mind that we had never been south of Inverness before, the excitement generated by this trip becomes more understandable. We dreamed of it for weeks beforehand; we read up about the various sights we might be privileged to see; we listened eagerly when our mother told us of things she had seen and done when she had stayed there with a family to whom she had been governess. The Castle and Princes Street Gardens with the famous flower clock were, I know, high on our list. But over and above all this we had one over-riding aim – we were determined to taste, for the first time in our lives, fish and chips.

Auntie Kate, an older sister of our father's, and her two daughters came to stay in our house, to enjoy a holiday in the glen and to look after the hens and the cat. I remember very clearly the sunny morning on which we left. As our aunt and cousins were seeing us off, they jokingly asked 'Where should we go to see this famous monster of yours?' 'Try a walk to Temple Pier,' said Dad, laughing. Then we set off on the great adventure.

Of the journey south I remember very little, except that another 'first' for us was staying in a bed and breakfast establishment in Perth. The realization of the fish and chips dream, however, remains clearly imprinted on my memory! We had reached North Queensferry and, finding that there was some time to wait for the car ferry (there being at that time no road bridge) we had parked the car and were looking around, when Nan and I espied a small, attractive-looking restaurant nearby. Our parents must have realised that they stood no chance! In we all trooped to have a delicious meal of fish and chips. It was to be several years, all the same, before we tasted them again. After this it was on to Mussel-burgh, to stay in a large and pleasant house near the sea with cousins of our mother's; during the week that followed, we went boldly into the city each day to visit places of interest. The one I recall most clearly is the Shrine, the War Memorial at Edinburgh Castle, where we were eager to look up the names of our father's two brothers killed in World War One; actually finding them, all the same, was a sobering experience.

The homeward journey altogether escapes my memory. What I do recall vividly is the arrival home; as always after an absence, our first thought was reunion with the cat. But this time an unexpected excitement awaited us – Auntie Kate and our two cousins were there to greet us, and they had seen the monster! They reminded us of the day of our departure when they had, with total scepticism, asked where the beast might be seen, and Dad had flippantly suggested Temple Pier. To Temple Pier they had accordingly gone, simply because they wanted a good walk, and there – along with a bus-load of folk, without a camera between them – they had seen the monster. No vague sighting this, either, they assured us; no tree trunk-like shadow far out in the dark waters of the loch, but a huge beast 'like an upturned boat', with a long neck and reptilian head, quite near the shore. And they had watched it for several minutes! They couldn't stop talking about it. Nan and I felt very jealous; why had we, who lived in the place, never seen it? Over the years, we would often urge our aunt to re-tell the story; she would oblige only if no sceptics were present! But when she did, it lost nothing in the telling.

It was the thirties, the time when 'monstermania' was at its height. Frequently the newspapers would report sightings in detail; some of these would be by local people whom we knew well, and knew to be of reputable character. One family in this category, living just above the loch, actually reported having seen two monsters at the same time. Other viewings were vague and distant, and easy to discount; still others were merely mischievous, by rascals whom nobody – certainly nobody local – believed for a moment. One such was a notorious playboy who allegedly saw the monster crossing the road with a sheep in its mouth; later he was forced to apologise to the newspaper concerned. Another tale, involving a different kind of apology (for which I cannot vouch, but it went the rounds of the glen for some time) concerned two American officers during the war, who had spent some time in the bar of the local hotel making fun of all the monster stories. Having left, on their way to Inverness, they saw the beast themselves, and returned to apologise to the regulars.

For our part as a family, it was the personal testimony of our relatives, particularly in view of their former total scepticism, which could not fail to convince us; added to this, we were well aware that stories of 'the beast in the loch' had circulated in the glen for a very long time.

A word about 'characters' – of whom there seemed to be many in the glen in those days, in comparison with today – although as children I feel we tended to take people's idiosyncrasies for granted. One of these was Sandy Ross, known as 'Sandy the Pier', pier master at Temple Pier. At one time glen folk would delightedly exchange 'send-ups' of the monster, one of which I remember well. Sandy was reported to be in the habit of telling tourists who asked endless questions about the monster 'Man, it's that big, it has to come into the bay to turn!' Many stories were also told about an elderly man called Donnie Fraser, known as 'Donnie Bullburn' from the location of his house. Because he was a small, wizened man tourists tended to make fun of him – but they reckoned without his rapier wit. One day, apparently plagued by stupid questions, when asked whether Gaelic was not his usual language he replied 'Yes, but we speak English to our dogs!'

What we could not know at the time, of course, was the extent to which this monster would, so to speak, dog our footsteps in the years to come, until we would become heartily sick of the sound of its name! Early on, as students, we learned *never* to say we came from Drumnadrochit –

it was always 'near Inverness'. Many years later, though, there came for me a great day of retribution. Having by then become a keen hill-walker, I was staying at a small hotel near Loch Lomond, where mountaineers of all grades foregathered; along with other regulars, I was enjoying the privilege of having tea in the private sitting room of the owner, an elderly lady who ran the hotel with her two daughters. Talk had turned to the monster, and I was enduring the familiar barrage of jokes about water kelpies, and about the increased likelihood of sightings around the New Year. As usual I was attempting to give a cool impression of not caring whether they believed in the beast or not. Suddenly the elderly lady, who was highly respected to say the least, said in a quiet but authoritative voice 'My family and I have seen the monster – twice.' There was a complete, stunned silence. For me, it was a moment to be savoured.

AUGUST

IF ANYONE, during our schooldays, had asked us what was special about the month of August, I can just imagine how our faces would have lit up as we answered that it was the time when the heather is out.

The heather – how important it was to us! To those unfamiliar with a rural Highland background, it must surely be difficult to understand this strange – but indisputable – dominance of the natural world in our young lives; just as surely as bird-nesting was our over-riding passion during April and May, so during August our minds would be filled with longing (and plans) to 'get to the heather'.

Achieving our desire was not altogether easy. The entire face of the glen was then cultivated, and it was only after you had climbed to the very top of one of the numerous tracks or farm roads – which might mean some considerable distance – that you reached the beginning of the heathery moors. In our case that usually meant either one of our holiday trips to the west, or, at home, being allowed to be away for several hours on a Saturday.

I remember so clearly the thrill of lying on my back among the heather, looking up at the wild sweep of the sky, drinking in the honeyed scent and listening lazily to the droning of bees. All the beekeepers transported their hives to the heather to produce that most rich and delectable heather honey. I would think to myself that heaven must surely be like this!

Because of the distance involved, and because in those days parental leisure time tended to be severely limited, I scarcely recall a single family outing to the heather outside the holidays. One expedition, though, I do remember vividly. Three families of children, with mothers only, set off to climb Creag Nay, a rocky hill to the north-east, for an all-day picnic. On such (rare) occasions there generally had to be a specific aim, which in this case was gathering blaeberries for jam. We found an area of coniferous trees under which the berries grew thickly, and there busied ourselves for the first hour or two, picking eagerly until we had filled several pails of the rich fruit – and had stained our hands (and tongues) a deep purple. This was always the way in those days: first you completed the work, and then you were free to enjoy yourself.

Then it was time for relaxation and refreshment. We children ran about collecting sticks for the fire, while our mothers started up a good blaze in a safe place, brought two black kettles to the boil and set out a variety of sandwiches and cakes. But first we had our special treat – a bottle of 'real' lemonade, as opposed to the kind our mothers made. I still remember those bottles with the strong metal clip, and the flavours available – still orange, still lemon, cream soda, ginger ale, lemonade, and a red concoction called cola, long pre-dating today's ubiquitous Coke. Afterwards, hungry as gannets, we tucked into the food, washing it down with that inimitable smokey picnic tea.

Only one thing in any way spoiled excursions in the heather, and that was the fear of snakes. I tend to think that Highlanders have always harboured a fear of adders, and I share it, hating to have my eye light on the sinuous coils of one. I would flee from it, however, rather than do it any harm. Many non-poisonous grass snakes must have had the misfortune to share the adder's fate in those days, for they were invariably killed. Adder tales – some of them almost certainly apocryphal – abounded in our family. There was the time Uncle Dave was bitten; his treatment consisted of drinking a large tumblerful of whisky, after which apparently he was none the worse. Then there was the occasion when Auntie Jan's precious cocker spaniel was bitten on the leg; she excised the area, sucked out the poison herself, dressed the wound, and took him all the way by train from Achnasheen to Dingwall, where the vet pronounced him fit and well and commended her for saving his life. This story I know to be true.

Sometimes on a hot day, when the presence of snakes was considered likely, we were made to wear our wellingtons for walking through the heather; although we chafed at this, it did make us feel safer.

The month of August often began, for us, in a distinctly unheathery place – Dingwall, on the east coast, where we would spend a holiday with our grandparents and Aunt Darla. Highlights there tended rather to be of a more towny nature, generally having to do with shops – and above all, the ice cream café. Just a short distance from the bottom of our grandparents' large garden there ran the railway line; at least once every day, provided we heard the train in time, we would rush out and wave a dish-towel, and to our delight would often receive return waves from several passengers and, best of all, sometimes from the driver. He might even pay us the supreme compliment of giving a special blow on the whistle for our benefit. This train, known to the family as the 'Westie Boy', was of great significance to us, for it was heading for Kyle of Lochalsh and passing on its way places we knew well – Garve, Lochluichart, Achanalt and Achnasheen, with which our family had close connections. Nan and I were crazy about 'the West'; we loved the wild places, and I can still conjure up with ease the special feeling associated with these, a kind of amalgam of heather and bog myrtle and hill lochs and, I admit, midges and fine smirring rain. We called that very common kind of day 'an Achnasheenie day'. To us it most certainly meant people as well, and – in our estimation at least – people who were incomparably

Aunt Darla, our mother's younger sister.

warm and welcoming, and who simply showered us with kindness.

When 'the Westie' passed during the Easter holidays, then, we would feel wistful because we knew we would not be going west ourselves; in the summer holidays, our hearts would turn over with excitement because we knew we *would* be going, the very next week! The pattern was always the same; Nan and I would be taken over and left in Dingwall for about a week, and then our parents would join us and stay for perhaps a weekend. Then we would all set out together for the exciting journey to the west.

Possibly the notion comes purely with hindsight, but I do believe we sometimes felt a twinge of guilt for our impatience to be off, in view of all the kindness we received at the hands of our grandparents and beloved Aunt Darla. The Sabbath, though, could be some-thing of a challenge! Granda was an elder in the Free Church, a good and kind man but of a stern mould; although he could often have a twinkle in his eye, we were always very much in awe of him – an awe greatly intensified on the first day of the week. The whole family of three generations would march to church in dignified procession in the morning, afterwards consuming a hearty meal (cooked on the Saturday); thereafter we would spend the day indoors, whatever the weather. The only books allowed were the Bible and *Pilgrim's Progress*. We chose the Bible, not only because there was one with pictures, but because *Pilgrim's Progress* scared us stiff. In addition, there was in our bedroom a picture of John Knox which Nan had, from a very early age, asked to have turned to the wall, with the plea 'I'm afraid of that angry man looking at me!' It was duly turned.

By the evening, however, all gloom would be dispelled; the grown-ups would all return to church after an early supper, and we would be left alone with Granny. Now she, while also devout, had an altogether different kind of personality; she was simply full of vitality and an irrepressible sense of fun. Unfortunately for her, we had early realised that we could manipulate her. No sooner had the adult procession left the house than we would rally to the attack. 'We're hungry, Granny!' On being asked what we fancied, we would invariably reply 'Please could we have bananas and cider?' Sure enough, she would produce them. Although the cider was in tiny glasses, it seems surprising that it was permitted; perhaps she regarded it as a kind of lemonade? Even today, a whiff of a certain brand of cider can bring back this memory.

This aim accomplished, we would proceed to the next. 'Tell us a story, Granny'. Often it would be a Bible story, followed by some incident from her childhood in beautiful Strathconon; having been born in the 1860s, she was not far removed from the Clearances that had been perpetrated there. She could hold us spellbound; it only added to our interest that she had to stop to think of the right English word, for Gaelic was always her real language. Granny was an ardent Jacobite – not surprisingly, for Flora MacDonald (the heroine of the 1745 Rising) was her great-grandmother's first cousin.

One Sunday night we ran into deep trouble. Somehow we had slipped outside and were under the strawberry net hunting for juicy specimens when a sharp whistle startled us; there was Granda, tall and erect and distinctly forbidding, standing there watching us. I cannot recall what was said (I am sure we were speechless anyway) but our tender-hearted aunt was detailed to spank us later. I'm sure we never dared to do such a thing on the Sabbath again!

Perhaps the sheer contrast with our own father contributed in some measure to our awe of our grandfather. I doubt whether anybody could have been more good-natured or have had a greater sense of fun (and of the ridiculous) than Dad; his ready wit was never unkind, though, and he laughed at himself more readily than at anyone else. To be fair, Granda could tell a story against himself as well! When my mother was young, the whole family either walked or went by horse and trap five miles to church each Sunday from Lochluichart to Garve and back. One day they happened to come upon a tinker lad gathering sticks by the roadside. 'My boy,' Granda said sternly, 'do you not know what day this is?' Quick as a flash, the boy replied 'Necessity, sir, necessity!' Granda told this anecdote more than once, clearly appreciating the boy's sharp riposte. Even he would concede that 'works of necessity and mercy' were allowed – at least sometimes.

Often before the big trip to the west our parents would take us from Dingwall on a visit to our Uncle Dave's sheep farm near Strathpeffer. He was married to our father's sister Hal (Harriet). They had no children of their own, but had a wonderful way with us. Both loved animals, and to our delight there would often be kittens of various sizes around the farm; only those classified at 'house cats' though, were catchable, as the barn cats fled from us frustratingly. For years, too, Auntie Hal had a black swan called Beauty, which had simply arrived one day out of the blue on the mill pond; it was so tame that it would often follow her around. We were more than a little scared of it.

Uncle Dave never seemed to sit down without having a collie lying at his feet; he – I mean our uncle – was tall and straight, with piercing blue eyes; an ex-soldier, he was proud of the beautiful sword that hung on the sitting-room wall, found in a bog nearby and allegedly having belonged to a redcoat officer. I think he was probably disappointed that Nan and I regarded its cruel, shining blade with nothing but horror.

He was another story-teller. His tales often concerned the prophecies of the Brahan Seer; the one which we found most fascinating was that which foretold that a cow would calve on the top of the Fairburn tower (not many miles distant); this was fulfilled when a cow apparently followed a trail of straw step by step to the top of the tower, and there produced her calf.

One year's visit stands out in my memory because, along with two nieces on Uncle Dave's side who were roughly our own age, we 'put on a play' in the big barn. Of its content I have no recollection whatsoever; certainly the inspiration, the directing and the decor must have come entirely from the other two, who attended the infinitely more sophisticated Dingwall Academy. We had only seen one play ourselves – *Macbeth*, performed in our public hall by a group of itinerant players.

Still, I do remember the thrill of being allowed to take part, and even the refreshments Auntie Hal provided in the barn at the interval.

A day or two later the car would be packed, we would say our goodbyes and the annual 'progress' to the west would be under way. Dad belonged to Achnasheen, about thirty miles away and today perhaps a journey of three-quarters of an hour. We all knew, however, that because of the poor single-track road and more especially the numerous stops ahead for visits and cups of tea, the journey would take the best part of the day. Until we reached the village of Contin, Nan and I were not the least bit interested in the scenery – orderly fields, houses and gardens; after that, though, things would look up, as increasingly these gave way to stretches of heathery moorland on both sides.

Before we reached Garve, we would come to the Rogie Falls, which we regarded with both dread and anticipation – the first, because of the very steep incline, which was an undoubted challenge to the cars of the time and not helped by the general absence of adequate fencing above the gorge below; the second, because if our parents judged that time permitted, we would stop and make our way down the winding path to the falls and stand watching until we saw at least one salmon leap upwards, always a beautiful and exciting sight. We hated the narrow swing bridge, though, preferring to stand a safe distance from the boiling water below.

Then, at Garve, the visits would begin in earnest. Our mother belonged to Lochluichart, a scattered yet amazingly close-knit community five miles west of Garve. The distance from there to Achnasheen, incidentally, was 12 miles; that was the distance cycled each way in an evening by Dad each time he visited her in their courting days! In Lochluichart, our grandfather, before his retirement to Dingwall, had been for many years head gardener on the estate there, and in later years a sheep farmer. Between them, our parents knew just about everyone in the entire area, or so it seemed to us; before the day was over, we would lose count of all the houses we would have visited. While Nan and I would quickly reach the stage of being unable to face yet another cup of tea, biscuit or scone, no such easy let-out was permissible for our father and mother, since a refusal of hospitality might cause offence. I believe it slowly dawned on us that although the glen was 'our' place, this area of Wester Ross was clearly theirs. Looking back, I now marvel at the close ties demonstrated and the faithfulness with which they sustained them; many of those visited were elderly, and would have been middle-aged when our parents were young.

The first visit would be to 'Sandy the Bees', in his cottage surrounded by a lovely garden and rows of beehives. We paid several other visits in Garve, but none which sticks in memory more vividly than that to 'Murdo Cnoc' (*cnoc* is a small hillock) and his wife. At some point Nan and I had noticed how very bare this cottage was; I recall that we asked about this, and our parents' explanation was that Murdo and his wife were very poor, subsisting on the productions of their diminutive croft. And why? Because they had consistently refused to accept a penny of the Old Age Pension – theirs by right, of course, but perceived by them as charity. Although a strong spirit of independence certainly did prevail in the Highlands at that time, I doubt whether there were many taking as brave a stance as this. They were a quiet, dignified old couple and their welcome was warm in the extreme. Our mother always gave them a present of half a pound of tea; she told us that to give more, as she would have liked, would have been likely to cause offence. They would have been self-sufficient in eggs, potatoes, vegetables and such like, but tea would be a luxury. Nan and I never forgot that pair.

There would be more visits after we had 'done' Garve. In Achanalt, we would pay a visit to the MacRae family, and would have to be shown again the tiny school where our mother had taught. And then, late in the afternoon, we would at last reach the scattered community of Achna-sheen, dead tired and in need of proper food after all the cups of tea, to

The house Dad grew up in at Achnasheen.

be welcomed by Uncle Jimmy and our three aunts. Mary, Becc and Jan were all known for their good looks but, as was commonly the case in the wake of the massive loss of life in World War One, had never married. Auntie Jan did eventually marry later in life.

I remember every detail of the Achnasheen house. It was of unusual shape, being composed of two cottages joined together so that there was a long corridor running along the front, and two staircases. Our family would be given the top flat at the east end, with two bedrooms and a bathroom; Nan and I couldn't wait to have our first bath there, being fascinated by the brown peaty water, after, that is, having been reassured in early years that we wouldn't emerge brown all over. After a huge meal and some talk round the fire, we would sleep like felled trees in the soft feather beds.

Everything, it seemed to us, was different in Achnasheen. For one thing, the mood was relaxed and nobody demanded anything of us; we were free to indulge in our favourite occupation, going up the hill at the back of the house to search for white heather, which we found without fail every year. Then the aunts would bring out an ancient, heavy black kettle and an old pot of the same uncertain vintage; armed with these, we would make our way to the shallow burn which ran down the hill near the house, and for hours would play happily, either making 'soup' in the pot, with cut-up rushes for leeks, or constructing temporary dams. We never tired of these games except on those occasions when the local midges – a fighting breed – would send us tearing indoors, almost frantic as they invaded our very eyes.

Uncle Jimmy, our father's oldest brother, who died when I was 10.

Uncle Jimmy with his bagpipes.

All the same, the really great event of the day was the passing of the 'Westie Boy', I think around noon. As the time drew near we would race down to the post office, some 100 yards distant, where Auntie Jan was post-mistress; we would sit quietly in a corner, watching fascinated as she

At Mossford farm: Granny, Nan on cousin Ann MacPherson's knee and Maisie on mother's knee.

and her staff sorted letters and parcels, stamping them at incredible speed and flinging them into the appropriate sacks. Those unfamiliar with Wester Ross may well wonder why a small place like Achnasheen should boast such a busy post office. This was because it was the rail-head, the parting of the ways; the railway went on from there to Kyle of Lochalsh, while buses carried passengers and mail to Gairloch and also, branching off at Kinlochewe, to Torridon. There would therefore be separate mail bags for the different communities on the western seaboard and the mountain-girt villages of west Kinlochewe.

When the time of the train was imminent, Nan and I would be away out to wait for that arrival of the wonderful steam train; nothing, to us, could have been more thrilling, and it was our perpetual regret that in our home area the railway had never come further than Fort Augustus – if only someone had had the initiative to join that line to the Inverness one! MacBrayne's buses were all right in their way, but could never hope to be that exciting.

Among the passengers alighting there would be, often enough, one or two who had some time to wait for their bus. Not infrequently these would make their way to the nearby MacKintosh house to be entertained by our aunts to tea and scones. Not many years ago in Aberfeldy I fell into conversation with a delightful old lady whom I diagnosed from her accent as being from Wester Ross; within 10 minutes it had emerged that she had regularly travelled, in her younger days, by train to Achnasheen and thence to her native Torridon, spending the waiting time with my ever-hospitable aunts. Uncle Jimmy had even played his pipes at her wedding! We remained firm friends until her death.

On at least one evening during our stay there would be a musical evening in the house, at which our mother would sing, Dad would play his fiddle and Uncle Jimmy would play the pipes. This last item was, to us, something of a mixed blessing. We knew he was an accomplished player, of course, and we liked the tunes (apart from the pibroch), but hearing the bagpipes indoors was a real assault upon the ears. If it happened to be in the bigger sitting-room at 'our' end of the house, it wasn't so bad; in the tiny parlour at the other end, we found it scarcely bearable – although we would never have dared to show our discomfort. But we really enjoyed it if he played out of doors.

On one day Dad would always be allowed a day by himself to go to the west coast, usually to Gairloch, for a day's sea-fishing; invariably he would return with a huge haul of haddock, plaice, codlings, and even a crab or two, but never, in those days, mackerel, which were dismissed as 'dirty feeders'. All of these fish would soon be shared with friends in the surrounding area. He clearly enjoyed his day, but we always felt that in a way he rather despised sea-fishing as being too easy; 'real' fishing was his great joy, and many a time we saw him come in proudly after an evening on neighbouring Loch Rosque with a basket of gleaming brownies – superior by far in his eyes! Even the midges failed to deter him.

In our own wanderings, more than once we came across the pathetic ruins of an old cottage – in some cases no more than a rickle of stones. I clearly recall the emotions these stirred up in us; incurable romantics always, we would build up pictures of the families who had once lived there. Our attitude would be one of wistfulness; never for a moment did we dwell upon the undoubted hardship of the life endured by the folk of former times. And yet, however one may smile at our romanticism, is it not possible that there was more to it than that – perhaps something of a 'folk memory' in these childish emotions? There was in any case an awareness that those who had inhabited such primitive dwellings were, in a real sense, our own people.

There would come at last the day Nan and I were waiting for; it would be our turn to journey further west. Granda had three unmarried sisters living near Ullapool, and each year we went to visit them. First we would go back as far as Garve, and from there take the Ullapool road, now a fine highway but in those days narrow and twisting, with passing places. Those old single-track roads gave rise to a special code of behaviour (described by one friend as 'the friendly bowing and scraping') in which whoever happened to be nearer the passing place would draw in and wait for the other car; passing, each would smile and wave. Unbelievably, one time when Dad had stopped and the other car was crawling past, he and the other driver, an Englishman, simultaneously recognised each other; they had been together in World War One! I have to admit that then, as now, the temptation existed to have an undignified race so as not to be the one to stop.

Before we reached the aunts, however, a huge treat lay in store. In those days, ordinary families such as ours never entered a hotel; eating out in our case was restricted to a very occasional lunch in Burnett's tearoom in Inverness. Yet on this particular night we would actually be sleeping in Aultguish Inn! This phenomenon is easily explained; the MacRae family who owned the hotel were long-standing friends of Dad's family. They were, incidentally, a well-known musical family in the North; one sister, Helen, was in great demand at concerts as a fine fiddler, while a brother, Hugh (a past pupil of our Uncle Jimmy's), was often to be heard on the 'wireless' playing the bagpipes. Aultguish Inn was run by the two youngest members, Mina and Donnie, a lively and interesting pair who treated Nan and myself like royalty. Before we had been properly settled in their private sitting-room, after the warmest of welcomes, we would be handed tall tumblers, decorated with salmon flies and brimful of lemonade; the adults would have tea and a dram. This was merely the first of a whole series of treats. Donnie would then allow us to open, gently and carefully, the many small drawers of a tall cabinet that held an astonishing collection of geological specimens – sparkling chunks of amethyst, smoky quartz (cairngorm), agates, garnets; we would be speechless with wonder. After a delicious dinner, we would – midges permitting – have a rare sight of our father having a cast in the nearby river before being ushered to bed in one of the comfortable bedrooms. Doubtless the adults talked far into the night.

Breakfast there was like no other. Porridge was served in small thick bowls, along with cups of very creamy milk, into which you were expected to dip your spoon half-filled with porridge. Then there would be oatcakes and honey; more than this I do not remember. What I do know is that staying there was one of the chief thrills of our young lives and, despite the fact that we were about to proceed westwards, we were very sorry indeed to go.

When it comes to recalling the circumstances of our next visit, to our three elderly great-aunts, a whole host of vivid impressions come surging back. They lived in a tiny old-world township called Achlunachan, a short distance beyond the (to us) quite terrifying Corrieshalloch gorge, again a very steep ascent presenting yet another severe test to the cars of the day, as well as a most daunting sight of the deep ravine lying far below the winding and largely unfenced road. This successfully passed, we could begin to look forward to an interesting – if not, to be honest, entirely enjoyable – visit to our mother's aunts, Lexie, Bella and Katie.

I believe that, even as fairly small children, we were aware that here we were stepping back into an altogether older way of life; indeed, to visit those three was to experience a brief encounter with the Victorian era. This was not simply due to their apparel – they invariably wore long black skirts to their ankles and high-necked blouses fastened with gold brooches – nor to the horsehair sofa that pricked our bare legs; it was simply apparent in everything, from the furnishings to the food.

Mention of brooches brings to mind an anecdote to which reference would invariably be made during each visit. During World War One our mother was employed as a governess with a family in Edinburgh. Knowing well the weakness of those aunts for sweet things, she used to save small amounts of sugar and syrup – then in extremely short supply – and every so often send a parcel of goodies to them. They never forgot this kindness. After the war they presented her with a beautiful silver brooch studded with garnets, which she was always careful to wear for the visits. Many years later, sadly, it was stolen from me on board a Cunard liner.

I think we were more than a little in awe of the old ladies. In their young days in the Highlands (in the mid-19th century), employment opportunities were almost totally confined to 'service' on the big estates which covered the area; their sole hope of advancement, therefore, consisted of aspiring to rise to the top of their chosen branch of service – to become head cook, housekeeper, laundrymaid – these posts carrying considerable prestige as well as real power over the numerous underlings, and much responsibility. This is what, we learned, each of the aunts had succeeded in doing, and a certain dignity still adhered to them. They would welcome us warmly, but had as little to say to us as we to them; as with everyone in those days, their principal concern was for our educational progress. After enquiring about this, and inevitably as to whether we had won any prizes, they would suggest that we might enjoy a walk up the hill at the back of the house. Nothing could have suited us better! Off we would go for the allotted time, without fail returning with

Granda with helpers at Mossford farm.

a bunch of white heather; everyone, in those days, took real delight in such a find, and much praise would be given.

We did not look forward to the meal, which would be set out on the finest china in the best room. I am ashamed to admit that Nan and I were finicky about food; the menu here never varied, and it was not to our taste. That we had to eat it, however, goes without saying. Several items happened to be our pet hates; we disliked salt venison (in itself surely a 19th century relic?); we hated strong tea, served with cream (regarded by the elderly as a delicacy); we were not at all keen on 'fresh' butter and crowdie (a type of quickly-made cheese produced on farms and crofts). In those days many, including the aunts, kept a single cow, and since the supply of cream was not plentiful, it would be some time before there was enough for butter-making; the butter would therefore have a slightly rancid taste. Luckily there would be some sweet things, which we liked very much.

On the whole we quite enjoyed visiting older folk; after enquiring about our progress in school, and exclaiming about how we had grown since last time, they would usually do one of two things – either offer us books to read, or suggest that we play out of doors. Either choice was welcome; we loved all books; we loved exploring outside. What we really dreaded was other children! To shy children like ourselves (and most Highland children in those days were undoubtedly shy), to be sent outside in the company of other, equally tongue-tied youngsters was sheer misery.

For the reasons outlined, we dreaded the visit we knew lay just ahead, on the return journey to Achnasheen. A gamekeeper friend of Dad's lived at Strathvaich, a beautiful, remote estate reached by several miles of rough track off the Garve-Ullapool road. There the father and mother, having accorded us the usual warm welcome and given us tea, would send us 'out to play' with their son and daughter, surely the shyest pair imaginable. We hadn't the faintest idea of what to say to each other! Happily each year the situation would be saved by their having some pet animals to which they would silently lead us; one year it might be a collie dog with *cuileans* (puppies), or a nannie goat with a kid. One year it was a pet stag. We were thrilled about this but our parents had reservations, and later in the car they explained why. Apparently, on the Fannich estate some miles from Garve the keeper had kept a pet stag, which became very tame and was always in the vicinity of the house. One day when he returned from a funeral the stag gored and killed him, presumably having failed to recognise him in his unfamiliar black clothes. I am uncertain when this tragedy took place, but my parents certainly knew the story well.

After this trip we would return to Achnasheen for the final part of our holiday; for us, it would be straight back to the burn and our black kettle and pot! In addition we became adept at weaving bangles and belts from rushes, which grew plentifully near the house. Thinking of such activities brings a reminder of the numerous games we played as children, simply making use of things growing around us – in the glen we had access to a much wider variety of vegetation than in the west. As small children, naturally, we made daisy-chains; we would spend hours looking for four-leaved clovers (Nan, who always had especially sharp eyes, even found at times five and six-leaved specimens); we used lengths of hollow-stemmed elder to make pea-shooters; we could whistle (or at least the boys could) through a certain type of broad-leaved grass; we collected spent cherry stones from beneath gean trees and used them for counting games and making patterns; we took pleasure in gathering oak apples and acorns (feeding the latter to a nearby pig); we played a game with 'soldiers' (the heads of plantains) in which the aim was to knock the heads off your opponent's stalks; the boys played a similar, time-honoured game with 'conkers' (horse chestnuts), while we girls – who never did get the hang of it – merely collected and cherished the beautiful mahogany-coloured polished nuts. There were certain flowers whose seed boxes made a satisfying popping noise when pressed; there were certain leaves (I think of the wild rhubarb) which, when placed upside-down in water, shone like silver in the sunlight... there was, in fact, no end to the amusements we could turn to whenever we were allowed the time to indulge in them. This was always the trouble in our case – never that we were bored, but that our all-important 'lessons' continually got in the way.

One cannot help wondering just how much of this satisfying country lore would have been missed, had we either had television or been supplied with the miscellany of sophisticated toys available to children today. There is no doubt that we revelled in our simple rural amusements; we were blessed in having an incomparable 'feel' of the countryside in which we lived; not only did we know it in a general way, but we knew every rowan and hazel tree, every wild raspberry and bramble bush.

Still, in an account which aims to be totally truthful, I must make an honest admission. One time in Achnasheen a youngish manager and his family had come to the hotel; we became friendly with the children and spent many happy hours playing together. They were very generous towards us and allowed us to play with their most cherished possessions – two pedal cars; on a large area of concrete in front of the hotel garage we took turns in pedalling happily. That year, our play in the burn was neglected!

On our final day in Achnasheen an event of extreme rarity in our young lives would take place – the aunts and Uncle Jimmy would kindly slip each of us either a florin (two shillings) or half-a-crown. This was riches indeed! We were aware, all the same, that apart from perhaps an ice cream or some sweets this largesse was destined for our piggy-banks and not for spending. Sadly then we would take leave of 'the west' for another year.

It was not, however, necessarily the end of holiday time; occasionally the whole family would have a week in a boarding house (in those days you had 'rooms with attendance' or 'rooms with full board'). This was very exciting. The destination might be either the popular resort of Nairn on the east coast, or Ullapool on the west – the latter then an old-fashioned village, possibly not all that different in size from the planned village built by the Herring Fishery in the 18th century – with no hint of the development yet to come.

In Nairn, everything centred on the sea and the sandy beaches; we were convinced we could smell the sea long before we reached it. Once there, we seldom left the sand, having no interest in the flat surrounding countryside. Each day, a bathe was obligatory; how anybody ever remained in that freezing water long enough to learn to swim is beyond my comprehension! I remember vividly the sinking feeling of undressing (in the seclusion of a bathing hut, naturally) and the correspondingly self-satisfied glow of returning to be dried, shivering, and being given a biscuit as a 'chittering-bite'. We would play for hours on end with our spades and pails, or 'pades and spails', as we liked to call them. Of our bathing apparel, what I remember best is that when we were small we had high-necked bathing suits and frilly caps like today's shower caps; we yearned for the more modern low-backed swimsuits, and used to gaze longingly into the window of the Nairn chemist's shop at their tight-fitting rubber caps with straps. The one good thing about not having such things was that when one did eventually acquire them, the thrill was great – so great indeed that I can still see those caps, one red and one blue, and smell the rubber!

The 'feel' of Ullapool was altogether different. But then, it was on our beloved west coast, and there were moors of heather all around, hill-lochs for Dad to fish, pebbly beaches on which to search (unsuccessfully) for agates, the pier with its strong fishy smell and an exciting array of fishing boats – and one year, the special treat of a trip to Tanera, one of the Summer Isles.

One thing that strikes me now about those far-off holidays is the almost complete lack of extra expenditure. Indeed it was treat enough for a family like ours to be enjoying a 'paying' holiday at all; extras were not even considered. If we ate out, it was at a picnic – and wonderful fun those were too. And in an age which knew nothing of theme parks, sea-life centres, interpretation centres or any of today's 'musts' for families on holiday, we had to make our own amusements. By and large, I believe we were delighted with them.

However much we enjoyed ourselves, all the same, there was always a special excitement about going home – first to the cat, then to the garden. I have the clearest memory of the first moments back at the end of the summer holidays – of going tearing up the garden to see how amazingly everything had grown in our absence; the carrots, turnips and cabbages would seem huge, the flowers would be everywhere luxuriant. Most of all, we would, if it was evening, long to smell the night-scented stock. It was always planted near our bedroom window, and as we were going to bed we would lean out and delight in the scent again.

It was good to be home.

SEPTEMBER

THERE IS A certain kind of early September morning which will forever remind me of 'back-to-school' days. There will be just a touch of frost, sometimes with a light haze giving promise of real warmth to follow; there may well be a whiff of burning from garden bonfires. This kind of day is associated with ripening apples, plums, hazelnuts and chestnuts, and certainly with chrysanthemums; above all, there is in the background the singing of robins.

What is now missing, thankfully, is that old sinking feeling in the stomach, that mixture of excitement and apprehension of going back to school, and getting into the rhythm of things again after the freedom of the long holidays.

Our school, let it be clearly understood, was never for the faint-hearted! Certainly it was a 'good' school, with a formidable and jealously-guarded academic reputation – understandable in the light of its small roll and location only 14 miles from Inverness – and it stoutly resisted down-grading. In any case the reputation was emphatically not gained through over-indulgence toward the pupils! From the earliest days, I truly believe, we were fully aware that school life was real and earnest. We were there for a single purpose; if we wanted to get on in life, then we had to apply ourselves.

Not only in the thirties but for a long time before, education was the shining goal toward which a great many Highlanders aspired. In a community such as ours the ministers, the doctor, the teachers and one or two other professional people formed a local meritocracy founded largely on education – although of course there were other worthy members who were also pillars of the community through sheer character and without recourse

Letter of recommendation for our mother.

to higher education. There was, incidentally, an almost total absence of class distinction (the gentry being so distant as not to matter). How could it be otherwise, when all came from the same roots? One telling example from the glen – although admittedly an unusual one – will suffice to illustrate the point; in a certain family one brother was a professor of divinity, another was a crofter, a third drove the baker's van. In those benefiting from higher education, any special airs would never have been tolerated.

We were more fortunate than we knew in having the opportunity for a good education so readily available. Never once, I am certain, did we appreciate this fact or even give it a thought. On the contrary, we took it entirely for granted that here on our very doorstep was a school in which we could remain, without even having to board a bus or spend a night away from home, until – all else being favourable – we left for college or university.

Our parents, just engaged, with maternal grandparents, 1921.

A brief look backward at the very different experience of the previous generation is, I believe, of real interest. Around the beginning of the 20th century people were generally very poor; education had either to be paid for or, if possible, achieved through winning bursaries. Families tended to be large, which meant that it was normally only the first one or two who were 'given a chance'; often the younger family members were expected to make financial sacrifices in order to help with this. As for girls, by and large they were not even considered; they had to make their own way. My mother had much to say at times about the position of girls in her own family – they had to clean all the boys' boots on a Saturday night in readiness for the Sabbath!

My parents' families were typical examples. Dad was the second youngest of 13! His much older brother Arthur studied law at Edinburgh University; the rest fended for themselves. For many in those days aspiring to work of some dignity and fulfilment, the Post Office (or much less frequently, the Bank) provided a reasonable answer; accordingly my father and three of his sisters underwent training in the Post Office. Dad specialised in telegraphic work – based on the morse code – in which he achieved high speeds. Employed at the outbreak of World War One as a counter clerk in Strathpeffer, he enlisted early and trained with the Cameron Highlanders in Inverness. On the very eve of departure to the

Edwardian group of mother's family. From left to right, back row: Rod, Ina, Duncan, The Maid, Dan. Middle row: Granny, Granda, our mother Eliza. Front row: Louis, who died aged 15, Darla.) Another child died in infancy.

Mother when she was a governess.

Dad in World War One.

trenches in France it somehow came out (he never knew how) that he was a trained telegraph operator; he was at once plucked out of his battalion and transferred willy-nilly to the Royal Engineers to serve throughout the war, in Salonika, with the Post Office. When, in family conversation, this story would occasionally surface, Nan and I would be totally uncomprehending as to why he had been anything but grateful for what seemed to us a providential escape, for a great many of his companions had been killed. But he had been ready to go with his unit, and was bitterly disappointed. Such, though, are the significant events that shape one's life; if indeed his life was saved through the agency of the Post Office, it was perhaps only reasonable that he should spend the rest of his life in its service!

My mother was one of eight. Her oldest brother, a brilliant scholar, won a classics medal at Edinburgh; the next brother became an architect; her older sister trained as a nurse and midwife. No funds being forthcoming in her case, she became a governess at around age 20 and taught in a couple of families before eventually being appointed a 'pupil teacher' at the small school in Achanalt, a few miles from her home, with 15 pupils aged from 5 to 15. How she managed such a mixed bunch was a mystery to us, but she always spoke of those years with the utmost enthusiasm. The fact that she also became a competent pianist after only a relatively brief period of tuition (the lessons paid for secretly by Granny, her father not approving of such frivolity) is a cause of pride for me, but also of shame in view of my personal failure to emulate her.

Mother – Eliza MacKenzie.   *Father – Kenneth MacKintosh.*

It was principally our mother, then, who was absolutely determined that, come what might, Nan and I should have the best 'chance' possible; although always a dignified person, she would not have hesitated, I believe, to go out and scrub floors in order to ensure our access to higher education. When, in our early teens, talk at school would sometimes turn to the dreams of certain girls of leaving school and getting a job, we never joined in; I don't believe we ever seriously wanted to leave, but we knew the idea was out of the question.

For many, school tends to be enjoyable in the early kindergarten days, and becomes less so as progress is made into the higher classes. My own experience was exactly the opposite; I found senior school full of interest and enjoyment, and left with considerable regret; yet having begun school with some eagerness at age five I became disillusioned almost immediately, soon developing what would now be termed school phobia. I am not sure how long this phase lasted, but I have an unhappy memory of being carried bodily into school, crying, and there was a period during which I was kept at home. I was a hypersensitive, timid child, suffering vicariously whenever a pupil was even shouted at, let alone punished, so that I grew more and more nervous. I remember how much I envied Nannie Stephen, the quiet friendly little girl who sat beside me, for her placid acceptance of the ups and downs of school life; how I longed to be like her! But for me, throughout primary school at least, waking up in the morning invariably brought a sinking feeling.

Disaster struck when I was only six. I recall clearly going home one day seeing 'two of everything'; I had developed a squint – brought on, the doctor claimed, by nervousness. Having to wear glasses may seem today a small thing; to me throughout my entire schooldays, it constituted a very real kind of suffering, effectively destroying any confidence I might have had in my appearance. The worst aspect – as for any child then or now – was simply being different from others. Having to wear those hateful round steel-rimmed specs was a sore trial! Then there were other things – being excessively careful during games; being called Specky (worse even than Skinny!); breaking my glasses in more than one fall from my bike; seeing myself, to my absolute discomfiture, in family photographs beside my pretty sister; enduring periodic visits to specialists – in pre-NHS days, at great expense to my parents. This particular trial was to last until at age 17 I went to an ophthalmologist who told me I had

Nan's school picture. Nan is in the third row, on the left, squashed in next to Mr Fraser.

no trace of a squint and that I should throw the hated specs away. I lost no time in doing so.

In school I soon settled scholastically, but for at least the first three years, not emotionally. There were just so many things to worry about! The classrooms, for example, had very high ceilings and tall windows which tapered to a point. I used to dread being the one asked to use the special pole for opening or shutting them from the top; even being called to write a word on the blackboard was enough to make my hands shake.

The lessons, all the same, and especially reading, became an increasing joy as time went on. Sometimes on a Friday afternoon we were given a rare treat, known as 'silent reading', when a cupboard containing all kinds of books would be opened, and we could choose what we liked. Such riches! The usual unrelenting rule of silence (the most common use of the belt was as a punishment for talking, and over the years I suffered twice for this) being for once lifted, pupils were allowed to exchange books with each other if they wished. How anyone could bear to do this was a mystery to me; it was agony to come to the end of the period having to leave a story unfinished.

At no time did numbers appeal as much as words; arithmetic was a task, a challenge, and never enjoyable. One painful memory is of something which happened on many mornings (not first thing – that was invariably 'Bible'), when we would be told to number from 1 to 10 down our page and thereafter, at top speed, would have to write down the answers to a positive barrage of mental arithmetic questions. The same would be done with spelling words, but that was nothing like as nerve-racking – I have to be honest and say I enjoyed it.

Even as very small children, it would seem, we took homework with the utmost seriousness. How often would our long-suffering parents be drawn in to help, in the dread event of a page having been accidentally blotted! How often, too, would either one of them be summoned by the plea: 'Would you put my arithmetic/grammar/spelling on me?' This phrase is a direct transliteration from Gaelic; it was to be many years before I even knew an English equivalent, when I heard my husband offer: 'Shall I hear you your homework?' As we went on through school, the burden became heavier; in the senior department we had an essay each weekend, a task which used to hang heavily upon us and spoil much of our enjoyment. Although the general rule was that it should be finished by the Saturday evening, more than once we had to rise very early on Monday morning – something which was absolute anathema to me – there being of course no question of our doing it on the Sabbath.

School life began to be transformed for me after the arrival of the Matheson family and the beginning of my close friendship with Joan. Having a best friend with whom to share lessons, anxieties, laughs, games and scrapes made a world of difference. During the latter years in primary school and especially during the senior years, our confidence grew steadily – until, I have to admit, in our final couple of years we were part of a fairly privileged group, and probably more than a little insufferable. I can still recall, for example, our being chosen to assist with the allocation of ration books early in the war and the self-importance of that honour – not to mention the thrill of earning our first pay of 10 whole shillings!

Having an older sister was, on the whole, no great bonus. At home Nan and I were more or less inseparable; school was different. It was made clear to me at the outset that, unless in dire emergency, I was not to call on her, and under no circumstances was I to follow her around. I think I tried hard not to disgrace her, especially on the two occasions when I was given the belt. There were two strict rules among the pupils in our school – never cry and never 'clype' (tell tales). On the occasions of my punishment, the sting of the belt took my breath away; I desperately wanted to cry, but I knew the rules – and anyway Nan would have heard! One day I did apparently disgrace her. Classrooms were divided by heavy partitions, and she later came home to tell me scornfully that from next door she had heard me read aloud in a high piping voice. Mortified, I lowered the tone consciously from that day on. It was while reading aloud, also, that the most embarrassing moment in the whole of my schooldays came about. I had been assigned a scripture passage to read that included the name of Mary Magdalene; to my horror I found myself saying my own name, Maisie, instead! Fortunately both the teacher and the class ignored the mistake, but it made me nervous of reading aloud for some time afterwards.

Cold winter days were, in the mornings at least, sheer misery for us. The large classroom was heated by a single coal fire; it would have been lit by the 'janny' much earlier, but would take at least a couple of hours to begin to emit anything like sufficient heat. Even then, the teacher would always stand directly in front of it! We would be frozen to the marrow, our feet blocks of ice (we all had chilblains) and our hands so cold that it was literally impossible to hold a pencil. By lunch time the fire would usually be like a furnace, which was just as well, because pupils who lived far from the school would have brought bottles of milk or cocoa (thermos flasks being then a rarity), which would be ranged along the front of the fire to be warmed up and drunk along with their 'piece' (packed lunch). No school lunches were available until several years later.

Nan and I cycled to school from when we started senior school, aged 11. We had learned to ride several years earlier, while on holiday at our uncle and aunt's home at Contin in Ross-shire. There was a large area of concrete near the house that was ideal for bicycles – which were unfortunately men's bicycles! Undaunted, we persevered until we could stay on reasonably well; fortunately our aunt was more tolerant of the black oil stains on our legs than our mother would have been! That holiday, I remember, was divided between two main pursuits – the bicycle craze and following around our older cousin, John, whom we greatly admired and on whose every word we hung.

For cycling to school Nan had an ancient, but excellent, Raleigh bike; mine was a Hercules, excitingly bought new, maybe to compensate for the endless succession of hand-me-down garments, but in performance nothing like as good. Free-wheeling, Nan would sail effortlessly past me. We were always at the last minute for school in the mornings; Nan blamed me because I was such a sleepy-head, and I blamed her because, hating porridge, she took such an age to eat hers. The result was that we had to go at top speed to avoid being late. The distance to school was about three-quarters of a mile. First there was a level bit past the hotel, and then began a long brae down over the bridge and by the village green. It was certainly just as well that our mother never saw the way we sped down this stretch without ever touching the brakes – thankfully there was much less traffic in those days. Then came a long hard haul – seeming perfectly flat nowadays in a car, but to us then a truly daunting incline, until we turned off the main road for the final straight to the school. We parked our machines in the school cycle sheds; there, from time to time, the air might be let out of the tyres by some of the boys, but otherwise no harm ever came to them. Our satchels of books were firmly strapped to a carrier behind.

We girls were, needless to say, at all times keenly aware of the boys in our class, although by my recollection there was little pairing off until around age 15 or 16. The more usual pattern was a kind of horseplay between groups of boys and girls in which, strangely enough, you tended to feel honoured if you were singled out for attack, and it happened to be your gloves or scarf that landed stuck up in a tall tree! The first sign of preference I actually remember is being offered, very excitingly, a share in a packet of Sun-pat raisins!

It is with a sense of reluctance that I approach the subject of teachers; perceptions being inevitably subjective, it is altogether difficult to be totally impartial. One thing, however, is certain, and that is that we were absolutely in awe of them. Meeting a teacher out of doors, boys were expected to salute, girls to bow. In stating that most of them were severe to a degree which would not be tolerated today – in some cases keeping an entire class in a state of fear – one has to add in all fairness that this was largely the ethos of the times. A teacher who didn't use the belt was something of a rarity – and possibly also looked down upon as something of a softie as well! Nevertheless, I do recall one or two who were able to achieve total co-operation through sheer personality and character, and who were deeply respected. On the positive side, it is worth making the point that it was simply taken for granted that we would be able to learn without noise or distraction of any kind, something which can scarcely be claimed in today's more liberal climate. Most punishments were light; but that some sadistic beltings could and did occur cannot be denied. Some teachers also tended to use sarcasm to an unacceptable degree; I can even, shamefully, remember a class being led in mockery of a stammerer.

There could be, at times, a decided lack of sensitivity – a single personal example of which remains in my memory even after all these years. Nan and I, then aged 12 and 10, had been allowed to go camping without our parents; this was unusual for the time, not least because few people in the glen would have possessed a tent. Indeed, we didn't either, but we were placed in the care of our older cousin Ann, an attractive, exuberant girl with whom we spent a wonderful week in a (borrowed) tent by the seaside in the Black Isle… until a veritable monsoon forced us on the second last day to send a telegram for our father to come and rescue us! Naturally on our first day back at school we were desperate to tell everyone of this high adventure. The teacher duly enquired of each member of the class as to how we had spent the holidays; proudly I told her. 'Camping?' she exclaimed in great surprise, 'without your parents? But you and Nancy are so precious – I'm amazed to think you were ever allowed!' I was mortified. Of course she was quite right; we were cosseted children, and I knew it. But her thoughtless remark wiped out most of the elation at a stroke.

What would be incomprehensible to children today is the fact that not only were we not permitted to talk to each other in class, but we were (generally, at least) not expected to ask a question, express failure to understand, or above all to 'speak back' – to attempt in any way to justify ourselves if accused. Despite all of the foregoing, it would be only right to add that there were many instances of kindness on the part of individual teachers towards children, especially those with problems – and probably a great many more of which we had no knowledge.

As the end of primary school approached, our entire horizon was shadowed by one particularly black cloud known as 'the qualy' (qualifying exam), which would later become the 'eleven plus'. The result of this daunting test would inexorably determine our course in what was then known as the 'Higher Grade'. In a small school such as ours, choices were severely limited; while the main subjects would be common to all, only the top stream would study both Latin and French, the next French only, and the 'dunces' technical subjects. There was certainly, at the time, a serious under-valuation of ability in, for example, woodwork, needlework and even art, in comparison with such subjects as languages or mathematics. As for those with real difficulties, such as dyslexia or deafness, they were all too often dismissed as stupid, and their chances of advancement must have been slim indeed.

Most of my personal memories of the Higher Grade are happy. French was my best subject; from the French teacher, Miss Chrissie Macdonald, I have to say that I received nothing but encouragement. In this I was, to be honest, more fortunate than some, for she was certainly no soft mark! She was, all the same, one of those who gave much help to pupils in need behind the scenes. As for her teaching results, it would be interesting to know for just how many years her entire classes achieved passes in Higher French. The language, dinned into our heads so many years ago, still remains remarkably in place, along with even the words of the French songs we learned to sing.

English and science were taught by Mr MacKell, later to become a popular headmaster. He was above all a superb teacher of English; to this day I can hear his expressive reading of such gems as Matthew Arnold's *Sohrab and Rustum* or the enchanting stanzas of Edward Fitzgerald's translation of *The Rubaiyat of Omar Khayyam*, much of which I still know by heart. Nihilistic as its philosophy was, truly the antithesis of all we were otherwise being taught, the beauty of the language delighted us.

> Oh, come with old Khayyam, and leave the wise
> To talk; one thing is certain, that life flies;
> One thing is certain, and the rest is lies
> The flower that once has blown for ever dies.

How he revelled in the Prologue to the *Canterbury Tales*, while we struggled with the mediaeval language! It was in our first year too, when we were concurrently coming to grips with the newness of Latin and French; yet his teaching brought it all to vibrant life, and if we did not

Miss C. Macdonald, French teacher, and Mr A.C. MacKell, English teacher.

emerge with a life-long love of poetry, it was certainly not his fault. Picking one's way painfully through Bacon's challenging, concentrated essays was admittedly somewhat less enjoyable, but it may have helped to stimulate our mental processes.

Mr MacKell's toughness as a teacher was at all times tempered by a keen sense of humour, examples of which would be relayed delightedly through the school by the class concerned. One well-known example will suffice. One boy, Willie Garland, always had a pocket watch suspended from a chain in his top pocket, and it was a habit of Mr MacKell's to flick this out with the end of his wooden pointer and ask: 'What's the time on your potato, Garland?' One day he flicked as usual and out came – not a watch, but a potato! That day the joke was on the teacher, and he enjoyed it to the full.

My personal memories of Latin are not happy – not because I disliked it, for in fact I took to it eagerly, and indeed in subsequent language studies have greatly valued its logical grammatical basis. But from the first day I entered her class the teacher, Miss Thomson (known as 'the Bird') took a dislike to me; as I had come timidly anxious to please, I found this hard to understand. It had something to do with Nan – just what, I never knew – for she would assure me again and again that I was 'just like my sister', for some real or imagined fault. I used to wish it had meant I looked like Nan! Looking back now, I realise that what hurt more than any punishment was the fact that she often disbelieved what we said; coming from homes in which telling the truth was taken for granted, we found this attitude incomprehensible. As the years went on, I lost heart and stopped working; our entire class, in fact, became totally unco-operative. This was perhaps a blessing, for at one time I harboured a desire to become a Latin teacher.

As to my attitude and that of my friends, while undoubtedly we had some just grievances, it is easy with hindsight to see something of the cruelty of which pupils can too easily be guilty. Instead of seeing this unfortunate teacher as dowdy, unattractive and spiteful, and I am sure she was aware that we did, we should have seen her as a person, a sad and lonely middle-aged woman looking after a difficult mother.

The headmaster, Mr Hugh A. Fraser, was nothing if not a complex character (and thus undeniably difficult to describe with total accuracy and fairness). He treated Joan and me with immense courtesy and friendliness when we carried out secretarial duties for him. A tall, powerfully-built man with an impressive embonpoint, in genial mood he could be said to resemble a large teddy-bear; in this mood at maths – which he taught to all the Higher Grade classes – he would prowl round while we sweated over some problem, humming to himself 'it's as easy, it's as easy, it's as easy as can be', to the tune of *Clementine.* He was not, alas, always this benign! If he should be in a rage, woe betide any who crossed him, even – or rather, especially – one of his own relatives. His nickname was Brochie (from Gaelic *broc*, a badger); word would then go round the school like lightning: 'Brochie's rubbing his ears!' The reason for this bizarre habit nobody knew; all we did know was that we were scared, and kept our heads down. At such times maths lessons were a nightmare. Personally I hated algebra and trigonometry, partly at least because their relevance and application were never explained, but fortunately Joan and I had somehow become adept at working out the various logical steps in solving geometric problems, which often saved our bacon. Girls were fortunate, though; Brochie was too chivalrous to belt girls, and this could often mean that the boys took an unjust share of the punishments. Once, though, during singing practice (he taught this as well) he exploded with rage at Nan for giggling and threw a pile of books at her head, shouting at her (for some obscure reason) that she would 'do better at a ladies' seminary'.

What we most dreaded was a Big Row. From time to time someone would have lost something – perhaps a torch, or a bicycle pump – or a window would have been found broken. Then there would be an inexorable inquest until the culprit had been found. We literally trembled in our shoes, having nothing to do with the matter. The worst episode of this kind I ever remember will make me feel miserably guilty until my dying day. A large group of boys and girls had been going up to the Public Hall, where we had gym each week, when something had occurred – I have no memory now of the details – which had caused somebody to be slightly hurt. A few of the older boys were somehow under suspicion, and several of us small girls were lined up to say – in answer to what was really a kind of rhetorical question – that we had seen those boys in a certain place. Petrified, having no idea of how to handle the frightening situation, we all to our utter shame said we had, when in fact all we had seen was a knot of people. I clearly recall being quite ill with remorse over this.

Despite those regrettable incidents, it would be true to say that we still had some fondness for the headmaster; in his kinder moments he could win us back. We also, I believe, came to realise something of his erudition and scholarship – although sadly, despite his being a Gaelic scholar, the language was never encouraged in the school. What did make a lasting impression on me was first of all his enthusiasm for the beauty of the *Book of Kells*; his teaching about archaeology also led to much enjoyment in later life, although I have never, despite much searching, managed to find a flint arrowhead or axe head, specimens of which he once showed us with great pride.

The education available to us in those days had its advantages and disadvantages. That the benefits were quite considerable has already been stressed – we had, on our doorstep, a school offering a sound academic education, free except for the cost of our books and certain educational materials. The books we used in the junior school were, I believe, generally purchased new. In the senior school, whenever we were due to go up a class there would be a great rush to beg or borrow the requisite texts from the class above; to shy children, this was a distasteful challenge. Here was one time when having an older brother or sister could indeed be an asset! As for the age of some of those books, today's youngsters would be astonished at what was acceptable to us – my copy of Caesar's *Gallic Wars* must have had the names of at least 10 former owners on the fly-leaf! Some of the names would go back years, names of people now married and with families, or long since gone from the glen. Not only was all this intriguing in itself; there was another bonus, in that some obliging forerunner would have written in the translation of some of the more obscure words. Clean, pristine volumes (which we had to have if we failed to find second – or tenth – hand copies) could have decided disadvantages!

Something which we, at least, considered anything but a blessing was the fact that we were 'pushed on' all the time. Pupils coming to join us from other schools seemed invariably to be well behind. This is not intended as any kind of triumphalism; it is merely fact. Early on in the war years, for example, a girl came to us from a boarding-school down south (her grandfather having once been headmaster of our school) to escape the bombs. Doubtless she could have taught us a great many things – about art and music, and certainly about games (she could even, to our intense envy in the days before the glen boasted a tennis court, play tennis!). All I remember, though, is that in English, Latin and especially maths, she was totally at sea; she also probably found us unappealing and incompatible, for after a single term she departed.

The disadvantages, then, must be apparent; we simply had a very narrow type of education. One thing which presented a real problem was the lack of choice. Literally the only subject option available to us in the senior school was between Latin and science; what if – at the age of only 14 or 15 – we chose wrongly? As it happened, Joan and I did (having inevitably decided to follow the same course together). Being language-orientated, we chose Latin. Having been influenced by a family friend newly returned from the United States to study for the rather new-fangled profession of dietetics, much later we found we should have had higher science, and thus required much extra tuition to pass the entrance qualification. All of this highlights another glaring lack of the times – we had no kind of careers counselling whatsoever, and not the slightest idea of the choices open to us. In our case it was even worse because there was a war on.

There was also a great deal less flexibility in education than there is today; here I refer to the system rather than simply to our school. I remember especially Helen Sutherland, an able pupil and later a close friend, who came from Ullapool to join us at the beginning of the second year; because there they had not begun Latin in the first year as we had, she was unable, to her regret, to study the language. There must have been many cases of this kind. Another problem was that, as the dreaded 'Highers' approached, we would be fearful of failing in those subjects in which we were weakest, because we believed (rightly or wrongly – and if wrongly, nobody ever told us otherwise!) that if we came down in one subject we would lose our whole group. In comparison with all of this, today's educational system – especially as regards university entrance – seems unbelievably flexible.

To return to the disadvantages of our own school, there was also the paucity of opportunities for games and general recreation. We girls did occasionally have a game of hockey, under the supervision of a gym teacher who came once a week from Inverness; we loved it, but it happened so rarely that we never reached any kind of proficiency. What I recall more vividly, unfortunately, is the bad fall from my bicycle caused by my hockey stick catching in the wheel! Perhaps the boys did better with football and shinty ('wild hockey'); certainly of the latter there was a very strong tradition in the glen.

With the single exception of literature, we were woefully ignorant in the realm of the arts. 'Art' itself, taken by the Latin teacher, could scarcely have been made more uninteresting, consisting as it did of a never-ending, and in my case abortive, attempt to draw the two sides of a series of jars and vases to match each other. Surrounded by beauty on all sides, we never once went out of doors to paint! In contrast, the vision of the primary teacher who had us draw a succession of wild flowers seems even more praiseworthy.

Music lessons, apart from those taken by some pupils privately, meant purely and simply choral singing, the standard of which was probably quite high. One feature of this singing teaching has left a legacy for which I have often had cause to be grateful – we were taught, very thoroughly indeed, by the medium of the 'tonic sol-fah'. This method has long since fallen out of favour, and is perhaps rather scorned today. At the start of every lesson, out would come the 'modulator' board, and we would have notes and scales dinned into our heads – or rather, our ears – which was fine for those blessed with a good ear; those lacking such a gift must have dreaded the 'ear tests' we would then be given. Nan and I were fortunate in our musical inheritance from both sides of the family; our mother drilled us in both staff notation and sol-fah. Soon we came to 'hear' any tune in sol-fah inside our heads, which made possible the instant noting down of any melody we wished to retain – in any place where we happened to have a scrap of paper handy. Perhaps, out of a great many possible examples, the most vivid memory is of sitting scribbling down the notes of enchanting Alpine songs in a mountain hut many years later, when we had become keen on folk melodies from around the world.

The range of musical instruments available in today's schools would have filled us with both amazement and envy – to think of actually handling a clarinet or a flute or especially a clarsach (small Celtic harp)! Of classical music we were sadly ignorant; even the briefest history of music would have been of immense value. It was not until student years that I began to realise something of the riches that had been denied us.

We could rattle off dates and quote from the works of many poets and novelists, but knew next to nothing of the great composers.

One personal regret, in view of a keen interest formed in later life, is that we were taught no social history. Ask us about wars, battles, kings; about the Armada, the Wars of the Roses, the Peasants Revolt; even – in Europe – such characters as Charlemagne, Richelieu, Bismarck, Garibaldi – we were at least on nodding acquaintance with them all. Yet we learned nothing of the exploitation of the Highland crofters, or the relentless repression of our own Gaelic culture; and it took my Granny to teach me about the Highland Clearances.

One final aspect of school life is the considerable group officially called 'boarded-out children', but called by us 'Glasgow orphans'. In remembering them I cannot escape a feeling of guilt. The guilt is first of all personal, not because of anything I did so much as what I failed to do, which is to make friends with even one, or take the trouble to find out how they felt about being transported to the glen. Were they really from Glasgow, or from a variety of urban areas? Were they really orphans? We had no idea. Perhaps there was some excuse, in that virtually all of them lived on the crofts and were thus not seen after school hours; all the same, we always tended to stay within our local group in school. And they were 'different'; they spoke with different accents, and dressed differently. On the whole, no doubt due to previous educational disruption, they tended to do badly at school, although there was certainly no lack of intelligence, and indeed some did outstandingly well.

I also have a sense of being part of a kind of communal guilt, in that as a community we did not, arguably, care enough about their welfare. Apparently 'orphans' had been coming to be settled on Highland crofts for many years before the thirties; their presence was taken for granted. To those of us brought up in the glen it was simply assumed, I believe, that they were very fortunate – they had plenty of good food and fresh air, and the chance of a good education. And certainly it was often noticeable that pale, thin children were putting on weight and growing rosy-cheeked.

Thinking of it now, my view tends to be different. For some, of course, for those who landed in good homes and were well looked after – and even loved – it might have been a good exchange. But what of the others, the ones who found the countryside alien and perhaps frightening? What of the ones who missed their mothers or their grannies, the neighbours, the chip shop, the games in the back courts, the teeming life of the tenements? To have to walk miles (sometimes in the dark) to some lonely croft might well have seemed to them extremely bleak – what would now be called 'culture shock'. Truly there must have been some in this position, for every so often we would be chilled to hear 'so-and-so has run away' – and that child would not appear in school again, nor would we ever know what had happened. In a day of much talk of human rights, one cannot help wondering how many they had.

One particular scene stays in my mind, not speculation, but well-remembered fact. One winter's morning, an 'orphan' boy in our class fell asleep during a lesson. The teacher was furious; she dragged him from his seat and shouted at him: 'How dare you, boy, fall asleep in my class!' Breaking the general rule of silent acceptance, he looked her in the eye and said steadily 'I'm sorry, miss, but I'm dead beat'. 'When did you get up?' she enquired. 'At half past five', he said. 'And what were you doing?' 'Bringing in sticks and peats, and cleaning out the byre'. Without another word she allowed him back to his seat. We all hoped she wrote to his fosterers, but we heard no more.

In straining to be fair on this subject, I should make the case, so to speak, for the glen folk. As far as the children were concerned, there was undoubtedly the extenuating factor of shyness; we would have been sensitive about asking questions about these children's backgrounds even had we been interested to know. As to the question of their being used as cheap labour, although the truth of this in certain cases cannot be denied, it was simply a fact that life on the crofts in those days could be harsh, and family members too had to work extremely hard. Finally, it must also be said that among the orphans there were sometimes delinquents; dealing with them cannot have been easy either for their fosterers, or for the welfare officers concerned.

There is a bright side to the story. That some were treated like members of the family is attested by the way in which many have come back, with their children and later grandchildren, year after year; their affection for the place and those who raised them is not in doubt. Others have stayed, married and raised families in the glen. To them and to their children it is home, just as surely as to those of us whose roots go much further back.

OCTOBER

WHAT EXACTLY was it that made October such an exciting month? First of all, the special feeling of excitement had to do with the quality of the weather; it was more marked on golden days, and was particularly strong out of doors, and in the evenings. As dusk was falling, we would be desperate to be out. Any excuse would do – there was some homework that would be best tackled in company, a song we had to practise, anything at all that we could think up. Sometimes it didn't work; we would be stuck at home. But even there, out in the garden in the darkness, there would still be that special feeling compounded of many things – the smell of garden bonfires hanging in the air, the stillness, the fallen leaves all around, the screech of an owl, the rising moon, the stars, the hint of frost – a mixture impossible to describe to those who have not experienced it, but instantly recognisable to those who have. To us as children it used to seem that on such nights all kinds of exciting things could happen.

Sometimes we would be allowed out to go and visit our friends at the manse. There were of course no street lamps in those days; we would have a small torch, but would almost never need it (and anyway it was necessary to save the battery); we knew every step of the way, and it never occurred to us to be afraid. Walking along past Drumnadrochit bridge – but not crossing it – we would see a row of glowing cigarettes, which indicated that the 'Drum boys' were sitting in their usual place on the bridge. They were a few years older than us and we were intensely shy of them (although they became good friends in later years), especially when they would shout wisecracks at us to which we had no repartee. Or they might well whistle a march tune in time to our steps. It didn't matter, though: we were brave in the dark.

We always called this type of October night a 'Hallowe'enie night'. The excitement reached its peak, of course, at Hallowe'en. But that must wait till the end of the month. Meanwhile there were other kinds of excitement.

One of these was the occasion of the Mod each October – this time the National Mod, or festival of Gaelic music, to which our mother always went. It was the only time she ever left us, and we enjoyed it – not that we didn't miss her (and the orderly running of the home), but we knew we could get away with much more with Dad, and anyway a break from normal routine was always a welcome diversion. She would be away for two or three days, being not only a member of the Glenurquhart Gaelic Choir (which would compete in the rural section) but also a competitor in several of the solo competitions; for many weeks before, she would have been at the piano practising the set pieces.

One particular Mod, held in Dundee, stands out clearly in memory. A telegram had arrived – we had no telephone in those days – to say that she had won prizes and was a finalist in the competition for the gold medal, judged on the aggregate of several solo competitions; she would therefore be singing at an evening concert. (She never did, incidentally, win the coveted gold medal.) Undaunted, our father fetched our good friend Greta to look after us, got himself and the car ready after finishing work, and set off for Dundee, a city he had never visited, nor was he familiar with the route. The effort, however, must have been worthwhile, for he often described the look of sheer astonishment (and delight) on our mother's face when she suddenly spotted him in the audience at the Caird Hall. Having driven back during the night, he was duly home and ready for work the next morning. Devotion indeed!

There was another quite different side to the month of October in the glen. To an extent which is quite unknown to most people nowadays, there was a sense of preparing for winter, of gathering in – an instinct which surely went back a very long way before our own time. It must have been much stronger, too, in the more remote crofts and farms than in us, mere village-dwellers only half an hour from Inverness; in days long pre-dating habitual relief operations by friendly helicopters, there was always a distinct possibility of their being snowed-in for some considerable time, and therefore of having to be stoutly self-sufficient. The extent of their preparations, as well as of their well-stocked 'kists' (chests) containing oatmeal and flour, would certainly have been greater than ours.

Visit to a nearby croft.

Our own preparations, all the same, seem quite significant in retrospect. First, in the garden provision would have been made for an adequate stock of those greens which would grow all through the winter, especially leeks, brussels sprouts, kail, and winter cabbage; also two deep pits would have been dug, one for potatoes and one for swedes, and covered warmly with layers of bracken. Much of our winter nourishment, then, would come from these six vegetables – potatoes, swedes, leeks, kail, sprouts and cabbage; in addition there would be strings of onions hanging in the shed and a large insulated box of carrots.

Potatoes were of absolutely vital importance for any Highland household, and particularly so during the war years. We used to have one week of 'potato holidays' (increased to two during the war) and they really were intended then for the school children to help in lifting – we never used the expression 'tattie-howking' – the potato crop. (Nowadays schools still have two weeks off, but few actually assist with the work.) In our own case, we had a goodly number growing in the garden; also, like most families, we had a drill in a field. Apart from the back-breaking nature of the work, there is to me a special thrill in unearthing the potatoes from the ground, especially if the soil is dry, and potato-lifting is a task I still enjoy. There is another side to it, though; sometimes I find it impossible not to think of the awful potato famine of the 1840s, of how our poverty-stricken ancestors had become so dangerously dependent on the potato, and of the stark despair which must have overwhelmed them when the dreaded blight appeared.

We usually, also, had a plentiful supply of cooking apples in our garden; these would be carefully wrapped individually in newspaper and stowed away for future use – a task we greatly enjoyed.

Then there were the eggs – what were we to do when the hens ceased to lay in the winter months? This was no problem! A special preservative would have been purchased, and a solution prepared in a large aluminium container; any surplus eggs, as they were laid during autumn, would be placed within this in a large wire basket fitted inside, and the lid tightly closed. The eggless winter could thus be faced with a considerable stock of 'fresh' eggs. Alas, I cannot say that I have entirely happy memories of them; somehow they had lost something – perhaps something more than merely the bright orange colour of the yolks – for they were never as acceptable as fresh eggs. But at least they were more popular then the ubiquitous dried egg of the war years, which set many a housewife and home economist racking her brains to find a reasonable adaptation of traditional recipes. The problem was never really solved.

In the kitchen we had a wooden 'kist', divided down the middle into two sections, one filled with oatmeal and one with flour. But it was surely our mother's larder which was especially worthy of note – and of sheer admiration! Scrubbed spotlessly clean and lined with paper, the shelves would groan under a wonderful array of jams, jellies, marmalade and chutney, along with a few jars of pickled beetroot, lemon curd and honey; these would not have the convenient metal lids of today, but would have been covered laboriously with gummed paper circles, each jar neatly named and dated. There might also be a jar of a certain 'tonic' made with lemons, eggs, cream and brandy, the eggshells having been dissolved by the acid to result in a mixture reminiscent of the Dutch 'Advokaat'. Many years later I had some students of nutrition evaluate this mixture, to prove that it contained every known nutrient!

Although we did not have – as many did in those days – a side of bacon hanging up, or a barrel of salted herrings, we did feel quite well prepared for winter; out of doors, too, we would have watched the stacks going up in the stack-yards, fascinated by the perfection of the work, although never at any time actually involved in it. Today's fat bales inside their black plastic sacks could never, one feels, stand a chance of rivalling the aesthetically pleasing sight of a neat row of stacks. Still, at least one can be thankful that oats, that most excellent of cereals, is still widely grown in Scotland.

Food in the glen was mostly simple and wholesome and, except perhaps during the war, plentiful for most of us. Even during the war years we were fortunate to have supplements – legal or otherwise – to the meagre rations. In our own case, having a father who was handy with both gun and rod meant we could enjoy such occasional delicacies as salmon, trout, venison and pheasant, while hares and rabbits were commonplace. All the same, during the war we greatly missed butter, cheese and bacon; also the lack of sugar, in days when jam and jelly-making was the only method of preserving a plentiful fruit crop, was undoubtedly a great hardship to the glen housewives – what they would have given for a freezer! I well recall the abortive attempts of my mother and her friends to concoct an acceptable jam or marmalade using saccharin and gelatine. We used to dream of the day when we would again have an unlimited supply of bananas and oranges.

Our day (weekday, that is) invariably began with porridge and plenty of milk. Unlike Nan, I loved it; porridge – preferably with cream – remains my all-time favourite food. We would often have oatcakes instead of toast as well, making our oatmeal intake satisfactorily high. (Strange that it took until the eighties for scientists to discover that this is a prime 'health food'!) During rationing, it was the butter for our toast and oatcakes that we as a family missed most; with our appetite for it, we could almost have used up the entire ration at a single meal. There used to be, I recall, a constant argument as to whether we should enjoy our measure of two ounces of butter on its own, and then put up with margarine for the remainder of the meals, or whether we should mix the two together, thus making it last longer, but spoiling the taste. The issue was never resolved!

The main meal of the day, whether at midday or in the evening, almost invariably followed a set pattern – soup, meat, pudding. No dinner was considered 'a right dinner' without these three essentials; there was in general far less flexibility than today. The glen housewives were great soup-makers, scotch broth, lentil, oxtail, leek and potato and cockaleekie being the most popular. Any of these could arguably have stood as a meal in itself! Pre-war main meals were based predominantly on the cheaper cuts of meat, as well as hares, rabbits, fowls and mealy puddings, while the subsidiary meals, whether lunch or high tea, relied heavily on eggs, cheese and bacon. Fish was regularly on the menu – not, as might have been supposed, obtained by poaching, but less colourfully by a van which came each Friday from Inverness, driven by a popular Italian called Polombo. Presumably Friday was chosen for the sake of local Roman Catholics; of these there was only one family in the glen, but he probably proceeded to Fort Augustus, and would have found many more there. We all bought the fish anyway. I have been told,

The grocer's van that called in the village each week.

although I do not remember it, that at one time he attempted a Sunday ice-cream delivery, but this was met with such general hostility that it did not last long. The glen housewives did well for vans, having a butcher's and baker's delivery as well.

Practically everyone in those days grew their own vegetables, and needless to say these were entirely organic, all gardeners worth their salt managing somehow to obtain a load of dung at some stage. Apart from potatoes, then, a main meal would generally include one or two vegetables in addition to those used in the soup. Of the few herbs used in Highland cooking parsley was easily the most popular, while mint and chives were considered a tasty addition to new potatoes in summer.

What today's children, used to ice-cream, yoghurt and mousse (not to mention Black Forest gateau), would think of the puddings of our childhood – rice, sago, semolina, tapioca, bread-and-butter pudding – is not altogether difficult to imagine! I have to say all the same that I loved them; it is fair to add, though, that our mother was always at pains to 'cheer up' a milk pudding, either by adding dried fruit such as currants, prunes or raisins, or stewed fruits such as apples, rhubarb or apricots. And highlights of winter menus were the steamed puddings: syrup sponge, apple dumpling and jam roly-poly, all of which met with everybody's approval.

Being to some extent finicky about food, both Nan and I were probably fortunate not to live on a croft. Fat meat was our particular bugbear; we often shuddered to remember the first time when, on a visit, we smelled sheep's head broth! I think we would both happily have become vegetarians. We also dreaded being given a 'treat' of a glass of milk warm from the cow. All the same, it has to be said that all glen children's milk intake was such that I believe the risk of osteoporosis in later life – today, sadly, a common condition – must have been minimal.

The glen housewives were great bakers, and our mother was no exception. Baking was of course strongly encouraged (and the standard doubtless improved) by the efforts of the Women's Rural Institute. Fancy items like cakes and meringues were generally for special occasions;

scones and pancakes ('dropped scones') were the order of the day. We loved the smell that would fill the kitchen when we came home from school to find our mother baking oatcakes and toasting them on the front of the range. Everybody who called would be given tea and something home-baked; it would have been considered a disgrace to offer a bought biscuit. There was one exciting exception – perhaps once a month or so our mother would have a shopping trip to Inverness, from which she would invariably return bearing a square carton from Burnett the bakers. We would be desperate to see what she had brought – usually either meringues or cream cookies. A red letter day indeed!

Although oatmeal did form a major part of our food, a great deal of white flour and sugar was also used – arguably the main nutritional fault in an otherwise very satisfactory diet. People generally had a 'sweet tooth' – although only a fraction of today's commercial products containing sugar then existed – and in this respect it would be fair to say that rationing during the war undeniably conferred certain health benefits.

The food on Sundays was altogether different. But then *everything* was different – and that by special design, for it was the Lord's Day, and nothing was too good to use in His honour; anyway, I believe that this was how my mother saw it. So we had the silver, the best linen and the best china, as well as a special menu. Nothing as common as porridge, then, for breakfast! We had bacon and egg, followed by rolls with butter and marmalade; and there would be a roast or chops cooking in the oven while we were at church. After the soup and meat courses would come the treat Nan and I were waiting for – which was in fact the only 'convenience food' of our entire diet – a packet jelly served with cream and, best of all, a tin of fruit; if this should happen to be fruit salad or cocktail, there would be keen competition for the single cherry! But on some Sundays there might be a trifle, and that was a treat too.

The parlour fire would always be on, and we would have our evening meal from a trolley; these were fairly novel at the time – in the glen at least – and our mother was proud of hers. There would be sandwiches of some kind to start with, followed by oatcakes or biscuits with cheese, and then some home-baked items and, except during the war, a banana.

The contrast with many of today's food habits in Scotland is nothing short of astonishing. To begin with, it was all 'real food'; whether you were making soup, macaroni-and-cheese or a gingerbread – anything at all – you began from the beginning and, step by step, made it for yourself. Tinned soups, for example, were freely available, but I would maintain that few housewives in the glen used them, except perhaps (as we did) a tin of Heinz tomato soup as a treat on a Sunday. And of course a certain number of baker's items were bought from Johnnie the Baker's, either from his shop in Milton or from the van.

On the other hand, it is in my view a good thing that today's menus are much more flexible – for example, it never occurred to us that soup along with a roll and cheese would make a perfectly acceptable meal; in those days, soup must invariably come at the start of a large meal. Nor did we ever dream of any other possible starter. Exotica like prawn cocktail or melon, or even grapefruit, were unheard of, at least by us. Undoubtedly, though, the greatest contrast as far as children are concerned is in the realm of in-between snacks; if we were hungry, we would be given a 'piece' – a scone or an oatcake, or bread and butter, or possibly an apple. The range of snacks on sale today – crisps, nuts, chocolate bars and sweets of every description – would have left us speechless, and as for the huge range of canned drinks... If we asked for a drink, what we got was either water or milk! Lemonade was a rare delicacy indeed. Having said all this, I cannot resist adding that our bones and teeth were almost certainly in a healthier state than those of many of today's children.

The autumn fruits were of immense interest to us. From early September onwards we would be sent out to gather brambles; familiar as we were with every nook and cranny of our immediate neighbourhood, we knew exactly where the best and juiciest ones grew. It was a task we found altogether enjoyable – apart from the inevitable battle with the thorns. We would happily range far and wide on a Saturday afternoon and return in triumph with a whole pailful of fruit, to be rewarded with, perhaps, a bramble and apple tart on the day, and succulent bramble jelly in the winter. Our father, too – not by any means the only male to undertake brambling expeditions from time to time – was once tempted by some laden bushes on a steep bank high above Loch Ness (well-known as a prime area for the fruit) and had a frightening slide which nearly landed him in the loch; he returned home as nearly chastened as he could ever be – but with his basket of brambles intact!

September and October were of course the time for apples. I must confess that in our early teens, Nan and I were involved in 'apple raids'. The term is simply a euphemism, for we knew very well that it was stealing; we knew also how distressed our parents would have been had they known. It was done, needless to say, more for excitement than anything else – which does not make it any the less shameful. We did not, above all else, want to be labelled 'goodie-goodies' – that seemed just about the worst thing that could possibly happen to us. It was bad enough already, since we were from a Free Church home, brought up fairly strictly and never usually in trouble at school. So we were determined to go with the crowd (peer pressure, it would be called today). But this was really only a symptom of the start of a rebellious phase, which also included experimenting with smoking (how we ever managed to get hold of cigarettes I have no idea; I only remember that we hid them in an ingenious place – the inside of an old box camera!)

Another of our acts of rebellion concerned the wearing of hats. It was unheard of for any woman or girl to go to church without a hat; in our anti-authoritarian mood, however, a few of us would remove our berets and hide them up the back of our coats as 'the crows' (black-clad wifies) came out from the Gaelic service, for the sheer enjoyment of being glared at. Obviously it was necessary to replace the missing headgear before we ourselves entered the church. All in all, at this particular stage of development I would judge that we were fairly obnoxious.

The thrill and excitement of autumn days – and especially nights – reached a peak at Hallowe'en. It is difficult to convey adequately just what this season meant to us; it was second only to Christmas in our estimation, and our anticipation as the day approached was such that it took precedence over everything else. Even in our work-orientated, disciplined school it was a wonder that the teachers got any work out of us at all!

For several weeks we would have been peering at the false faces in the window of the local shop, making our choices in preparation for the night, and we would have ferreted out a weird collection of garments with which to clothe ourselves; it didn't really matter what you looked like as long as you were unrecognisable. Very few then would take the trouble to 'be' a pirate, a gypsy and so on, except if there should be a party at someone's house – we used to dread having to go to one of these (as once, out of politeness, we had to do) if it should be on the last night of October and would cause us to miss the fun of guising! As for our parents, they would have laid in a stock of 'monkey nuts' (peanuts with their jackets on), hazel nuts and apples, as well as pennies and halfpennies; it would never do to disappoint the guisers.

There would be fireworks in the shop too (we called them 'sky rockets') but these played a fairly minor part in the celebration; we might be given a few pennies to spend on squibs, but the more exotic productions were beyond our means. Bonfires were not yet important either, although some extra rubbish and pieces of wood might sometimes be added to the necessary garden fires.

The excitement of Hallowe'en lay mainly in the fact that for once we were free to roam far afield with our friends; it was fun to dress up; for children who did not receive regular pocket-money, the financial advantages were not to be under-estimated either! (Nan and I once, I remember, came home with 11 pence each). I don't think anyone ever thought of it as begging; we always had to 'do our piece' – and anyway it was a tradition, and traditions were taken seriously. It is worth emphasising too that, certainly in our own experience, what may be called the occult overtones of today's Hallowe'en, in which children appear to be bombarded with spells, witches and spooky stories, were absent. True, we might well meet a sheet-clad 'ghost' in our travels; but all in all, it was an evening of simple fun.

At last the great moment would come and, clutching our turnip lanterns, we would be off. The weather was of prime importance, and in memory it always seems to have been fine – but we would have gone out anyway! It is easy even at this distance to recapture the feeling of excitement as we set out – and the sheer unpleasantness (not that it mattered) of attempting to breathe, and speak, through a false face that had become soggy around the mouth. From house to house we would go, first in our own village and then away over to Lewiston, the next village more than half a mile away. Some houses would be in darkness and disappointingly closed against us; we always had a good idea, though, of the ones where we would be welcomed. In we would file, to sing our song or recite our poem; then the real fun would begin, which involved the inhabitants of the house identifying each of the guisers. In a community in which most people were known to each other, this meant that our voices must be disguised as well – it was considered a disgrace to be recognised! Then, whether this had been done or not, out would come the largesse – and into our capacious bags would be dropped anything from nuts or sweets to jingling coins, and we would proceed happily on our way.

On the road we would often be passed by groups of guisers a great deal taller than ourselves, since it was by no means unknown for adults to join in the fun by going guising as well, sometimes taking a fiddle or guitar with them. Years later, I remember, Nan and I were at home from the city with a young doctor friend, to find ourselves at one point in the evening introducing her to none other than our local doctor, both dressed up, and both happening to be wearing false faces with enormous noses!

There was one other aspect of Hallowe'en, though, which is perhaps less well-known, and that is the tolerance (for that night only) of certain pranks which would otherwise have been strongly censured. It was rather like the observance of April Fools' Day. These were carried out mainly by groups of young men and, as far as my knowledge goes, consisted principally of removing gates, or sometimes blocking chimneys by climbing up and placing a turnip on top.

One occasion remains indelibly in my memory. Late one Hallowe'en night I was awakened around midnight by some sound and, my bedroom being at the front of the house, I got up and peered out, to see by the light of the moon a band of stalwarts in the very act of removing our gate from its hinges. Fascinated, and with never the least thought of telling my parents (despite the trouble my poor father would have in retrieving it) I watched gleefully as they quietly bore it away.

It must have been before we had a car, for there was an amusing sequel the following morning as our family were walking to church. At the precise moment when we were meeting another family marching to a different church, we suddenly spied a whole pile of gates, our own among them, stacked neatly on someone's lawn. The red faces of the two young sons of that family told a clear story!

NOVEMBER

THE ONE MONTH in the year which we would gladly have done without was November. I have before me an article by Nan and myself, written in the fifties from Canada at the request of the then editor of the *Glen Urquhart Bulletin*; after extolling the delights of the glen month by month we commented that 'even the glen used to seem slightly dreary in November'. That was indeed true, when what could normally be expected was a long succession of raw, damp, miserable days. More importantly perhaps, nothing interesting was growing outside – even the hens were 'off the lay' – and we were driven indoors, not just to our inevitable 'home lessons' and piano practice, but to find some solace in indoor games and, occasionally at least, crafts. It was in fact virtually the only time in the year that the outdoors lost its attraction.

Still, there could be exceptions. Sometimes, usually at the beginning of the month, there might come a brief spell of really fine golden days; these we would use to the full. Everywhere there would be fallen leaves, of every hue from gold to russet and dark brown, and through these we loved to 'scruffle' with our feet; if they happened to be really dry, many leaf-fights would take place, and we would be in trouble through being late home from school. Our mother made a different use of the autumn leaves. When they were first turning colour she would always gather a spray of beech leaves and preserve them in all their beauty either by putting them in a vase in glycerine, or pressing them for several weeks under a carpet.

It is when I think of autumn days that I am reminded inescapably of Tim. The nephew of our doctor's wife, he came to the glen in the later years of the war as a kind of evacuee from a public school down south, to live in the care of a housekeeper in a small mansion house owned by his grandparents. Despite what must have been a certain degree of culture shock, Tim took to life in the glen like a squirrel to nuts; he loved the freedom of the outdoors, and with his endless vitality and restless energy (today he might possibly have been labelled hyperactive) he was forever in search of new ploys – if it wasn't building a hut of branches, it was making catapults or bows and arrows or, at one time, a raft to float on the river. Or, inevitably, since Tim was never one to worry over-much about rules, it was organising apple raids. Undoubtedly he was possessed of considerable leadership qualities and personal magnetism; we had never met anyone remotely like him, and at least five of us girls had a huge crush on him, following him about like a little flock of hens. He could make us do daring things. How could I forget the rope which was suspended from the roof of the steading at Drumbuie Farm, only just reaching the hay-loft above? What Tim required was that we go up there, grab hold of the end of this rope and then, hanging on for dear life, swing outwards on it. This absolutely terrified me, but I did it rather than have to hear Tim's scornful 'coward!'

Going past our gate at high speed in the gloaming (he could cycle at night because, unlike us, he had a dynamo), he would give his customary salute of a long-drawn-out yodel; Nan and I would look up, delighted, from our school-books, while our mother, who like the other mothers thought him a pernicious influence, would remark that it was high time 'that boy' had a bit of discipline. True enough – he must surely have led the unfortunate housekeeper a merry dance at times.

Thoughts of Tim's endless zest for living make the fact of his tragically early death all the more poignant; it so happened that, years later, Nan and I were on holiday in the glen when, dying of cancer, he went back to say his farewells to the place he had grown to love like no other.

For our hard-working parents November doubtless offered something of a respite, since there were few tasks to engage their energies out of doors; still, there was never any lack of things to see to inside – like poring over the seed catalogues and planning their planting strategy for next spring. And, as in every other thrifty household of the time, and to an extent that would seem incredible to modern young people, there was an on-going, demanding programme of 'make-do and mend'.

Thrift and frugality! Those were the keynotes of the domestic life of pre-war rural Scotland, as habits were instilled into us which were to last a lifetime and – at least as far as I am concerned – were to afford deep satisfaction; I still abhor waste of any kind. Virtually nothing that could conceivably be used again was ever thrown out.

It began, I suppose, with food. At the purchasing end, much thought would first of all be given to what was good value for money; nothing 'trashy' would be considered. And every particle would be used – butter papers would be scraped, bags of lentils, barley, rice and sugar emptied to the last grain; marrow bones used to make delicious soups; extra fat on meat 'rendered' by heating in a frying-pan and pouring off the liquid for later use; much ingenuity would be employed in the use of any left-overs. But thrift entered into other departments as well. Tiny ends of soap would be made into soap-jelly for various cleaning purposes; parcels would require the string to be carefully unpicked, and kept, tidily rolled up, for later use. Our mother even kept a box of stamp edging for mending her sheet music – how she would have welcomed sellotape!

Frugality was practised just as much when it came to clothes. I remember so well the times when, some time during the winter, a dressmaker would come and stay with us for perhaps two or three days; she and my mother would be busy all day long with the sewing machine, planning and making things – some from new material, but much more from old; they would cut up old curtains, old coats and old skirts, out of which clothes for us would magically emerge. From the new material, most memorable were dresses of crimson velvet with cream lace collars; we really loved those dresses – which, to tell the truth, is more than could be said of all our garments.

Maisie wearing a dress made by the visiting dress-maker.

The linen cupboard would have its contents overhauled

A wartime cottage wedding which turned into a ceilidh.

at some time as well. Thinning sheets would be sewn up 'sides to middle'; any frayed pillowcases or towels would be carefully mended, while towels deemed past their best would be demoted to become floor-cloths or washing-up cloths. Mending was, in fact, going on all the time. Nan and I were taught to mend our stockings – how we hated that! And in school we were also taught to mend socks; the darns had to be pretty well invisible too.

During the war, with clothes coupons in desperately short supply, the utmost ingenuity had to be exercised by all the women, the local WRI being predictably to the fore. Hats underwent some mysterious process known as 're-blocking' – all of the wifies wore hats then, and not solely to church – while coats and skirts were turned, or dyed, or had fur collars added – anything to give them a new lease of life. I scarcely need add that, when any garment really had reached the end of its useful life, before being thrown out (and even then it probably lined the cat's bed or lagged a pipe) every button, fastener, and later, zip fastener was carefully removed to be used again.

It strikes me now that differences between the lifestyle then and now go much further than the degree of frugality practised in the way things were used; it is also to be seen in the number of things we simply did not have. One need only consider literally hundreds of products that today are commonplace in people's kitchens – ready-made sauces, pastas, cake mixes, tinned and frozen items of every conceivable kind, as well as a huge range of soft drinks; but also today's bathroom shelves laden with all manner of soaps, talcs, shower gels, deodorants and cosmetics. The list is endless. Most of these, it can be said with confidence, we did not have, and did not know we needed. Nor did we even dream of many things we find necessary today; imagine living without sellotape, plastic boxes, soft toilet tissue and kitchen rolls and polythene bags! Or imagine living through a hot summer without a refrigerator or a freezer! This last thought brings to mind my mother's method of keeping milk fresh, which was to stand the jugs of milk in a basin of cold water outside in the meat-safe, which had mesh walls to keep it cool and keep insects out, each jug covered with a circle of muslin weighted with beads and trailing in the water.

For our parents, leisure time was always in short supply. On Saturday evenings, though, or sometimes for a brief period between homework and bedtime, they might join us in some simple game. We had no sophisticated games, but derived endless enjoyment from Snakes and Ladders and Ludo; we also played Snap and dominoes. No playing cards were to be found in our house, although we learned to play whist while staying with an aunt and uncle. Dad loved to play tiddlywinks with us, and could beat us hands down every time. But most of all he was a wizard at draughts. Our mother was not interested in the game and we lacked the patience to learn, so we almost never saw him play; all we did know was that each winter he would be invited to play in some kind of draughts championship in Inverness, and invariably he would return with a most exciting prize – a hamper of delicacies that we could hardly wait to open. There would be a tinned ham, all kinds of tinned fruits, exotic cheeses, chocolates, crystallised fruits, an iced cake... all luxuries to us. We definitely approved of our father's talent for draughts!

There was an altogether different 'game' that we played all the time, and that was collecting cigarette cards. I no longer recall clearly whether all the makers went in for these, or which ones did; what I do remember is that every child we knew was a collector, and we constantly swapped cards in school, desperate to collect the entire set. The trouble, in our own case, was that we had no rich source to draw on – Dad smoked only two or three a day. We were thus thrown back on finding discarded packets by the roadside (yes, there were litter louts around then too; quite often a group of us would see a motorist throw out an empty packet, and there would be a frantic race to be first to pick it up). I can still recall the feeling of excitement as one drew out a pristine card, eagerly scanning it to see whether it was 'needed'. Finding cards discarded in this way was much more exciting, in fact, than having them tamely handed over. Our mothers all strongly disapproved, needless to say – after all, you never knew what 'germs' might lurk on a card. We were not deterred; the game went on for years. All this time later, the name of some flower learned from the cards (calendula) or some animal (armadillo) will bring back an instant memory of the game. Although we hardly ever went to the cinema, we knew the names of dozens of film stars!

Lest the impression should be given that the month of November was wholly given over to trivial pursuits, it should be said that, on the contrary, in the senior school it was exam time. Memory too easily recalls the whole tense atmosphere surrounding those exams, for which we worked feverishly – admittedly, too often during the final couple of weeks before, rather than throughout the entire term. We would be arranged at desks in 'the big room', first year pupils alongside fifth or sixth years in order to obviate copying; as the papers were handed out in total silence one's heart would be in one's mouth. Maths papers I always dreaded; practical tests in science would set my hands shaking. But to be absolutely honest, I looked forward to and actually enjoyed written exams in English, French and Latin – not that it would have done to confess anything of the sort at the time.

Once this hurdle was over there was a wonderful sense of relief. We could really start looking forward to Christmas.

DECEMBER

W HY IS IT that December always seemed an infinitely more
exciting month than November? I believe there were three
main factors. First and foremost, Christmas was on the
horizon. Second, there was a distinct possibility that we would have snow.
Needless to say, these two things went together; certainly we were
dreaming of a white Christmas long before we ever heard Bing Crosby
sing his famous song.

Third, there were the Christmas holidays to look forward to. Apart
from, perhaps, the final days of the summer term, there was no other time
at our school when a slight slackening of discipline could be sensed, and
even a lessening of the load of homework. The run-up to Christmas was
always an enjoyable period. All in all then, the two months were
essentially different in character; whereas November was an exam month,
December was to be enjoyed.

If the snow failed to come, though, December would still find us
leading our lives indoors instead of out; nor was there any lack of things
to occupy us, for our mother was firmly of the opinion that children must
be taught that it is more blessed to give than to receive. We therefore
learned to make presents for friends and relatives. What we actually did
make I find hard to remember – apart from our *pièce de résistance,* which
was knitted 'kettle-holders'. This item may well puzzle younger readers! In
a day of kitchen ranges and even open fires to cook on, the handles of
pans and kettles could become blisteringly hot, and everyone used
holders. We would knit colourful rectangles and then double them over
and sew up the sides; our mother would then crochet (an art we never did

View of Inverness.

acquire) a lacy edging in a contrasting shade, to finish them off. After having been carefully pressed they would look quite decorative; also – something which is quite important to a child – we knew for sure that they would be used.

During the war years, though, knitting for others became more of a necessity than an optional extra. There was in existence at the time something called 'Jock's Box' – an organisation through which service men and women received gifts. These probably took many different forms, but as far as the glen wives were concerned, their involvement meant predominantly the provision of home-knitted socks, and to this end many worked industriously during the entire duration of the war. Nan and I were accordingly taught to knit socks (including the daunting technique required to turn the heel); I do not recall whether we managed to produce many pairs, nor indeed how acceptable they would have been when completed. Perhaps more successfully, we also knitted endless blanket squares, make up of ends of every conceivable colour of wool; where they went to be sewn up into blankets, or who they were destined for, I now have no idea. To be honest, at least the fact that we were involved in producing them helped to satisfy the endless queries of one of our teachers as to 'what we were doing for the war effort'; in truth we were doing very little. When asked, we would drag in the fact that as a family we entertained the troops – these being in fact one or two members of the Canadian Forestry Corps, who had a camp a few miles down the loch-side. To us they seemed ultra-glamorous figures, mainly on account of their accents, which we constantly attempted to imitate – all the time wishing that we might be allowed to meet them socially at the local dances.

Dances, usually held on a Friday night in the Public Hall, were at the time emphatically not for us! But once we had reached our teens, we would occasionally be allowed to accompany our parents to a concert or *ceilidh*. By far the most exciting of these events was the annual 'dramatic concert', at which our local drama group would present three short plays. What the actual standard would have been is impossible to assess at this distance, but I believe there were some gifted performers; in our eyes, anyway, the whole thing was nothing short of magical. Some, maybe most, of the plays would have been comedies, and of these I have some vague memories, but it is in fact a very different one that remains sharply in memory, which centered on the search for fugitives after the Battle of Culloden, and in particular, on children being questioned as to the whereabouts of their father. This was an emotive subject in the glen, from which many had gone to fight and die in that ill-fated campaign; a local writer expressed it thus: 'The months after Culloden brought a misery and horror without parallel in the history of Urquhart'. That play, then, upset us deeply as children, and made a lasting impression; we could not dismiss it as make-believe, knowing even then its basis in cruel reality.

Normally concerts and *ceilidhs* were purely for enjoyment. The general absence of sophistication ensured that local performers were given quite an ovation, no matter how many times they had played the same tunes or sung the same songs; in our own mother's case, she would often prepare and sing new songs, but inevitably before she left the platform someone would shout out a request for her to sing one of her special Gaelic songs. There was no shortage of talent in the glen – singers, pipers, fiddlers, Highland dancers – although occasionally at a slightly grander type of concert reinforcements in the form of, perhaps, a Mod medallist, an elocutionist, a comedian or even a ventriloquist might be brought in from Inverness. For all that, it was the simpler *ceilidhs* we enjoyed most, since at these the seating arrangements would be more informal, as was the whole atmosphere, and in between the solo items there would be dancing. Sometimes, to our great delight, we would then be asked up for a dance – an eightsome reel, a waltz, Gay Gordons – best of all, with our own father.

Brought up in an area of outstanding natural beauty and with a keen interest in all the productions of the land – whether these were wild or grown in garden or farm – we tended to live most of our 'real' life out of doors, and in this we were fortunate indeed, for country joys last a lifetime. But at the same time we were coming to appreciate a whole range of activities intimately associated with family life. In an age before television, and with even 'the wireless' a strictly rationed commodity, we were obliged to make our own amusements. Above all, we had time for each other, and family relationships were close.

As children, then, it can truthfully be said that we were listened to, given advice, encouraged, helped with our homework (and, make no mistake, corrected, and smacked whenever necessary). Also, with a father like ours we had to put up with a great deal of gentle teasing; this was always a common feature of Highland life, and stood us in good stead in later years.

Books were always of prime importance, although our choices may seem strange to some. We knew nothing, for example, of some of the more popular children's classics such as those by Beatrix Potter, or Kenneth Grahame's *The Wind in the Willows*; we couldn't stand *Alice in Wonderland*, and although some fairy tales did appeal to us, certain ones in the Hans Christian Andersen collection we found frightening. We loved stories of adventure and initiative, such as *Robinson Crusoe* and *The Swiss Family Robinson*, as well as more homely tales, of which I remember best a series of girls' stories called the Katy books – *What Katy Did, What Katy Did Next*, and so on. (What she actually did I have now forgotten!) But our top favourite book – still extant but distinctly battered after having been through the hands of the next generation – is entitled *Wonder Tales of Past History*. In each story the child heroes, Peter and Poppy, rub a magic ring and find themselves flying back into some historical situation on the back of the Phoenix – an ill-tempered bird to say the least. No matter where they landed, whether in ancient Britain or ancient Egypt, they would be trapped in a sticky situation, but to our relief (for we couldn't abide sad endings) they would remember to rub the magic ring at the most dire moment and sure enough the old Phoenix would appear, grumbling, and bear them back to their own safe life. We never tired of that book; we read it over and over, and even learned a bit of history through it! One thing I do know – if C.S. Lewis's wonderful *Narnia* stories had existed in our time, he would have had two avid readers.

At no time were we given money to buy comics. However, by some means we must have acquired them (probably by swapping something else), for I have distinct and happy memories of the *Dandy* and the *Beano*; the former was our favourite, with Oor Wullie, Desperate Dan, Keyhole Kate and Freddie the Fearless Fly. On a single occasion we tried to copy a very inspiring idea. Oor Wullie and his friends, having found an old mattress and succeeded in fastening a spring to each of their feet, were able to go hopping about, sailing over all obstacles in their path. For days we combed the local dump looking for old bed springs; we did eventually find them, but were forced to abandon the idea – Wullie must surely have had wire-cutters!

Our mother never did approve of comics, but at one time a friend of hers kindly gave us a subscription to *The Children's Newspaper*, an altogether more edifying publication. Perhaps it was because of the element of compulsion – or a natural perverseness – but we disliked it from the start, and would only read it under supervision.

Thinking again of the joys of the hearth which winter always brought, I am reminded especially of our Sundays when these were enjoyed most fully. In contrast to the somewhat repressive sabbatarian atmosphere in our grandparents' home (which, however, owed nothing to our granny!) our Sundays were enjoyable at all times. True, they were quite strictly observed, and they were distinctive in their use of different clothes, food, linen, china and books. The parlour fire would of course be lit, and a 'scorcher' it would invariably be, providing a pleasant focal point in that comfortable room. Although our normal pursuits were not allowed, we didn't mind (we *did* mind in the summer, all the same). One thing we sometimes did as a family was to bring out the old psalmody books and sing in four-part harmony – our parents taking the soprano and bass, Nan and I singing the alto and tenor line respectively. We were all keen singers and we loved the metrical psalms; this is another pleasure which has lasted throughout life.

After our meal, which would be eaten from the trolley round the fire, Dad, as precentor, would have to accompany our minister for the evening service; in a rota, this would mean going either to Balnain, five miles 'west the glen', or to Bunloit, a scattered settlement high on a plateau above Loch Ness, or else to our own local church. Going to Bunloit in winter could mean a difficult, even hazardous, journey in snow; I can recall more than once their having to leave the car and wade through deep snow to reach the small school where the service was held. To have to turn from the fire and the warm comfort of home on such nights must surely have been a challenge for our father. I never once heard him complain.

For us, the evening would be idyllic. Our mother would read to us round the fire – sometimes stories from the Bible, sometimes from other books that passed the test of suitability. Then would come cocoa, and best of all, toast made on the glowing coals with the brass toasting-fork, which always hung by the fireplace. No other toast could compare with this! Finally, after prayers (which of course took place every night, not just on Sundays) we would go sleepily to bed. What child, indeed, would not feel altogether warm and secure after such a day?

In the run-up to Christmas, several events return vividly in memory.

One of these is an occasion known locally as 'Miss Burgess's Carnival' – Miss Burgess being a local lady with outstanding organisational gifts (not to mention the person whose primroses we had pinched). To Nan and myself, this carnival was tremendously exciting. For those used nowadays to all kinds of 'spectaculars' – whether in real life or on the screen – it will be quite impossible to imagine our feelings as we entered the Public Hall; familiar to us, yet now transformed into some kind of fairy grotto, blazing with lights, festooned with greenery and coloured decorations, and with everyone in the entire district (or so it seemed) milling around inside. The lady organiser required no tips from today's professional fund-raisers in the art of parting people from their money; still, much enjoyment was had by all at the same time, and anyway it was all in a good cause – in support of our local hospital, the Royal Northern Infirmary in Inverness. In pre-NHS days, this was taken very seriously.

What we ourselves took most seriously was how exactly to get the very best value out of the sixpence (a fortune) we had been given to spend. There were just so many choices to make! If, for example, we were to spend it all at the stalls, which would be groaning with sweets, small cakes, toys, mistletoe, decorations and especially 'tablet' (fudge) which was sheer delight to us – there would be nothing left for the other attractions. The thing was that it was just possible that by these we might actually go home enriched... by a coconut, for example, if we should have a good enough aim; or we might have success at quoits, or hoop-la, or the bagatelle board. Or it might be by clever guessing – the weight of a cake, the number of sweets in a jar, the name of a doll. We knew better, though, than to try to beat the local housewives at seeing how many clothes-pegs we could fix on a 'washing-rope' in one minute! We were usually keener to try to drop our penny to land, hopefully, on top of a florin (two shilling piece) or a half-crown, which sat alluringly in the bottom of a pail of water – although I never saw anybody actually do this. Better, certainly, to keep the penny for the Lucky Dip, a barrel filled with bran in which all sorts of toys lay buried.

As the entire proceedings were conducted against a background of noise – not only of talk and laughter, but also the blaring of toy trumpets and ear-splitting blasts on penny whistles – it was small wonder that we would be tired out as we trooped homewards clutching our loot. We wouldn't have missed it for the world – it was an exciting feature of Christmas, which by then would be just around the corner.

Another special occasion, when we were old enough, was going to Inverness on a pre-Christmas visit with our friends from the manse –

All dressed up for a visit to Inverness – Nan, Joan, Rena and Maisie.

Maimie, Rena and Joan. This was naturally much better than going tamely in a car with the family. It meant a journey full of chatter and laughter on MacBrayne's bus, and being chaffed by the driver, who would be a familiar figure to us all. Everyone knew and liked the local bus-drivers – Alec 'Shillings', Sandy ('Sandack'), and Jock 'Seanair' (meaning grandfather). What we most admired was the amazing way in which, without stopping the bus, they could all aim a rolled-up newspaper and have it land on a person's front lawn, or even doorstep. Often though, they had to stop, to deliver a parcel – or some chickens!

Having reached town, we would make a beeline for Woolworths. Spending our money there was like the carnival all over again – choices to be made between sweets, jewellery, scent and tree decorations. At last, decisions made, we were off to our next port of call – the Rendez-vous, an Italian café beside the River Ness, there to spend what was left of our money on a great delicacy – a raspberry sundae. This was the most exotic treat imaginable, every mouthful to be savoured as slowly as possible.

From about mid-December onwards, there was nothing in our heads but Christmas. It need hardly be stressed that the ethos of the day was light-years removed from today's materialistic, stressed-out extravaganza; all the same, for us as children it was simply the most thrilling thing in the entire year. It would make a good story to be able to say that we were intent on finishing the gifts we were making to give to friends and relatives; the truth was that we were primarily concerned with what we would receive! Perhaps there was some excuse in that it was an age in which few gifts came our way other than at this one time.

I can clearly recall lying awake – especially if there should happen to be snow – thrilled to the marrow imagining Santa Claus beginning his journey from the far North with his galloping reindeer. Exactly how he was to get down our chimney was a question which exercised us quite considerably; in the end, though, we were content to leave it. Alas, my 'believing' ended abruptly when I would only have been five or six, when someone told Nan the awful truth, and she of course told me. I used to feel quite resentful that she had enjoyed two whole years more of believing than I had! Actually I refused at first to countenance the very idea that Santa didn't exist – until, one evening, we wickedly went and searched the bottom of the spare room wardrobe and found mysterious parcels hidden there.

Sometimes on the Saturday before Christmas we would have a party – the usual simple, genteel little tea with our friends (invariably girls), with one special addition to the tea-table; prized above all else, we would have a circular box of crystallised orange and lemon slices. It is debatable whether it was the taste of the slices or the tiny metal three-pronged fork which pleased us more! Failing these – and almost as popular – we might have a box of dates.

There would follow a variety of games – blind man's buff, hunt the thimble, dominoes; at some point, too, our mother would come in to play the piano for musical chairs or pass the parcel. One of the simplest games, but perhaps the one which gave rise to the greatest hilarity, was called 'Poor Pussy'. The idea was for the one who lost the toss to pick someone else and try, by 'miaowing' in the most pathetic and harrowing way, to make that person laugh; if she failed, and the victim was able to reply with a straight face 'poor pussy' each time, she had to keep trying, but that didn't often happen. Another game which caused much laughter was consequences – mainly because we would find local characters placed in wildly unlikely situations. It wouldn't have been nearly so funny had we not all known them so well.

One Christmas a few of us were invited to a party by a wealthy family who lived (at least occasionally) in a large and beautiful house about three miles 'west the glen' from us; it has been a hotel for many years now. What I remember best is the excitement of the approach up the long driveway, and seeing a tree near the front door lit up with coloured lights. This means little today; bear in mind, though, that at the time most folk in the Highlands did not have a tree at all, let alone coloured lights; as for a tree *outside* being lit up, that was simply a taste of fairy-land!

It is strange how, out of a whole episode, one's memory will selectively retain only one or two specific points; I recall, for example, nothing of the food, which is likely to have been fairly spectacular. What I do remember is the treasure hunt – the first we had encountered – which took us all over the house; they must surely have been most tolerant hosts! What remains most clearly in memory is that one clue took me to 'the pink bathroom'. A *pink bathroom*! Never could we have imagined such luxury; colour co-ordination was not a preoccupation in Highland households of the day. I remember finding the clue pinned to the most opulently soft pink towel I had ever seen – and there were pink tiles too, and even a pink carpet. A carpet in a bathroom! In our strictly utilitarian bathroom – and we were fortunate to have one – linoleum and a rug were considered sufficient.

Interestingly, I do not recall that this very special party in any way spoiled our appreciation of our own simple little celebrations. We did perhaps hope that the invitation would be repeated another year, but the family probably spent few Christmases in the glen, and it never was.

In view of the fact that Christmas was, in the thirties, still an ordinary working day in Scotland, and that many of the older folk of the glen did not actually celebrate the festival at all (nor would some of the children receive any presents, except perhaps at New Year), I marvel now that our own parents made it so very special and exciting for us. We even had a small artificial tree, with coloured glass balls and some tinsel, which was brought out every year.

As with Easter, though, there was little sign of the true meaning of Christmas in our preparations, the Free Church resolutely refusing to 'name a day' for the birth of Jesus Christ; rather, His coming was an event to be remembered with gratitude all year round. Being taught from the Bible at home, in school and in church we were naturally familiar with the account of the nativity; I recall little mention of its relevance to Christmas. True, in school we were taught carols, both in English and French; sadly we knew nothing then of the lovely Gaelic carol by Mary MacDonald of the Isle of Mull, celebrated now as *Child in the Manger*. The clear favourites were *Once in Royal David's City* and *Away in a Manger*. But the one which most appealed to me was the non-biblical *Good King*

Wenceslas; I would lie cosily in bed conjuring up the scene – the benevolent king with his page trudging valiantly through the 'deep and crisp and even' snow, to bring gifts of 'flesh and wine' to the poor peasants. Partly, of course, it was the vivid words which gave delight, but the scene did allow the imagination free rein, and it was very satisfying to a child. I still love it.

One really surprising thing was that in school – no doubt because of exams being over – there was actually a distinct relaxation in the tempo of work; we would even be allowed to make and colour Christmas cards. Again, I very much doubt whether these ever included scenes of the stable in Bethlehem – not that my feeble artistic talents could ever possibly have aspired to such heights! Instead, firesides with stockings hanging up, plum puddings and holly were more than sufficient for me.

But the holly – how much that meant to us! By far the most memorable part of the season for us was being allowed to go with Dad to get the holly (in earlier days we had no other decoration, apart from the little tree). It was always the same place – a small farm called 'Tigh Chat' (cat-house) high on the brae past Temple Pier on Loch Ness. There were several holly trees growing there, at least one of which could be relied upon to have berries – naturally it was essential to find some 'berried holly'. Probably we were more of a nuisance than anything else, for we could not ourselves cut the prickly bits of holly, but our ever-tolerant father put up with us and I believe he enjoyed it as much as we did. Three things combined to make that outing very special: being with Dad; seeing the dark shining waters of the loch stretching far into the distance beneath us; and the fact that it was Christmas Eve. We did not then, as now, decorate our house days in advance. Then it would be home to supper, followed by an impatient wait until it was time to go to bed and hang up our stockings.

Did I say stockings? Here I must make a shame-faced correction, for it was actually a pillowcase that Nan and I hung up. This may seem surprising in view of our generally modest way of life, but is easily explained; our parents always added the parcels that came from relatives and friends to their own. In the earlier days this did admittedly puzzle us – how could Santa manage such a thing? Well, it seemed he could and we accepted it as a fact.

How we ever slept at all is a mystery. For one thing, we would be absolutely determined not to; we wanted to see all! But sleep would come; and, as with children everywhere – even sleepyheads like us – we were up with the lark. I shall never forget the incomparable thrill of stretching one's toes down to the bottom of the bed and feeling the crinkling of paper; then, with trembling fingers we would be digging into our pillowcases, unwrapping the parcels (no bother at this point about rolling string and folding paper!) and finally reaching the small things at the bottom – the inevitable tangerine, a bar of 'tablet', a pencil.

Yes, we were fortunate. But precisely because this was a unique occasion, the thrill was undoubtedly enhanced. The plethora that surrounds most children in this country today would have astonished us. Is it not at least arguable that over-abundance can even become a kind of deprivation, removing as it does at a stroke much of the pleasure and elation?

So it is that I can still remember with the utmost clarity some of the gifts we were delighted to receive – nightdress cases (we always had these at the time) in the shape of shaggy dogs, with zip fasteners down their middles; handkerchief sachets (another requirement of the day) one in pink satin, one in blue – Nan always had pink and I had blue, no matter what! And one year we were given 'Dorothy bags' – sewing bags in soft leather with tiny containers holding needles, thread and scissors; I have mine still. There were also things to wear; it was many years before I learned that in more affluent families these were considered dull and unacceptable. We, on the contrary, would be thrilled to receive slippers, gloves and scarves. One never-to-be-forgotten year our parents gave us dancing-pumps with shiny metal clips at the front – such opulence!

After breakfast, having been supervised as we tidied up and put away every vestige of wrapping and string, we would be away post-haste to the manse, to share our Christmas news with Maimie, Rena and Joan; clearly it added to the excitement to have friends with whom to compare gifts. One year stands out – when the green fingers of envy reached out and touched us – for they had each received a watch, no less, from their wealthy aunt and uncle in London. A watch! This was the very epitome of luxury, the stuff of dreams; we had longed for one for years. (As it turned out, I had to wait until I was earning my own living.) We didn't have a wealthy aunt and uncle; but we did have cousin Jessie, a teacher, who was always extremely generous to us, and that year, fortunately, she had sent us the doggie nightdress cases; generously, the girls came back right away with us to admire them.

After all this there would be a fine dinner – special, but never quite on the scale of the New Year one – and then Christmas Day would be over. Inevitably there would be a sense of anticlimax. Perhaps we would begin reading a new book, or play with some of our presents. Then, after cocoa by the fireside, we would go to bed deeply content. Strange indeed had we not been content! Who could possibly have asked for more?

INDEX